George H Moss Jr

DOUBLE EXPOSURE TWO

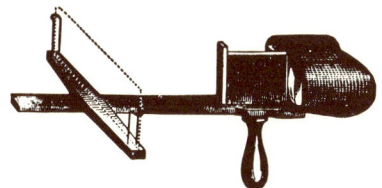

DOUBLE EXPOSURE TWO

Stereographic Views of the Jersey Shore (1859 to 1910) and Their Relationship to Pioneer Photography

George H. Moss Jr.

with a foreword by
Lee Ellen Griffith, Ph.D.
Director
Monmouth County Historical Association

Sea Bright, New Jersey

For
Mary Alice
...still in the picture.

and for
Wilfred D. Howitt
...who made it all possible.

Copyright © 1995 by George H. Moss Jr.

This book, or any portion thereof, may not be reproduced
in any form without written permission of the publisher.
All rights reserved.

Library of Congress Catalog Number 95-071818
ISBN 0-912396-07-5
Printed in the United States of America

FOREWORD

Like no other branch of the early photographers' art, the stereograph possesses the ability to bring its era into sharp focus not only through the images that it presents but also by the nature of the stereographic cards themselves. This delightful medium and the method by which it is views satisfied the Victorian fascination with gadgetry and science, while the range of subjects reflects the eclectic culture of the nineteenth century. The power of stereographs to truthfully speak for their age lies in the great number and variety of subjects captured by the stereographers' three-dimensional process and also in the candid nature of many of the images. While early photographers produced carefully posed portraits of many now-nameless ancestors dressed in their finery, the stereographers more often sought out subjects in the process of living, working or playing, resulting in a more direct and revealing picture of the times.

As twentieth-century viewers, we must first appreciate the impact of the art and science of photography on nineteenth century culture and understand its mass appeal. In a sentimental age, an appreciation for the realism of portrait photography may be expected. "It is not merely the likeness which is precious...but the association and the sense of nearness involved in the thing...the fact of the *very shadow of the person* lying there fixed forever!" So wrote Elizabeth Barrett Browning in 1843. An issue of MacMillan's Magazine, published in London in 1871, described "the array of little portraits stuck over the labourers fireplace" and the social benefits that photography could provide by "counteracting the tendencies, social and industrial, which every day are sapping the healthier family affection. The sixpenny photograph is doing more for the poor than all the philanthropists in the world." That is quite a testimony to the importance of photographs and their universal availability in that early period. Among other social benefits that may be ascribed to photography are education and amusement which would be found in the Victorian parlour by looking through a stereoscope.

The special significance of the stereograph as part of late nineteenth-century material culture is evident in the pages of this book, Which allows the stereographs themselves to reveal all kinds of information about their subjects, their makers and the people who purchased them. The author's own tireless detective work and detailed analysis of the images and the cards to which they are affixed serve to amplify those images and to give them a context that will enable readers to better perceive their meaning. As presented in this book, the stereographs are not only nostalgic images of the past but significant cultural artifacts. All aspects of the stereograph as a historical object are explored here, including the stereographer's name and advertising information printed on the back of the card which can yield valuable information about marketing practices and often can locate and date the photographer or publisher's place of business.

The stereograph and the stereoscope that brought the images to life were more than just a clever Victorian parlour amusement for their owners. They served as souvenirs of leisure activities, documented historical events and landmarks, commemorated or memorialized special events, and some that were published in series were documentary in nature. The choice of subject matter and popularity of certain views, like Grant's Cottage at Long Branch, allude to the cultural preferences and interests of the photographers and of their customers; for example, the preponderance of beach scenes and images of hotels among the known stereographic views of Monmouth County underscores the economic importance of the tourist trade summering at the shore in the second half of the nineteenth century. The in-depth section on stereographic views of Monmouth County, drawn from the collection in the Moss Archives, creates a rich and complete vision of the region in one period of time.

This particular collection has been recognized for its values to local history by an exhibition at the Monmouth County Historical Association, "Optical Delights: Stereographic Views of Monmouth County," and by grants from the New Jersey Historical Commission. Through their support, the images from the Monmouth County stereographs have been reproduced as a study collection, which is now available for public use as part of the Monmouth County Historical Association's Library and Archives. Much of the life and spirit of the stereographs is in the detail of their images, and much of the historical data can be found there as well. Leisure activities, vernacular architecture, interior decoration, business practices, public events, dress and style are but a few of the topics that might be explored through this study collection to the benefit of local historians and those investigating the broader social history as well.

Those of us who study and interpret or just enjoy learning about the past have a wonderful and unique resource in this collection, which is remarkable for its scope and volume. Nowhere is there a comparable collection of New Jersey stereographic views. In the years since George H. Moss Jr. published the first DOUBLE EXPOSURE, he has continued to explore the topic of stereographs, to identify their makers and to refine and expand his collection. The result is a vivid picture of local history and culture that has become richer as new pieces of the puzzle fall into place. The clarity and immediacy of these stereographic images speak clearly for their subjects. Equally intriguing and equally important is the opportunity to look past the images to their makers and discover a thriving industry linked to tourism and leisure time, a new and evolving concept in the Victorian era. Arranging the stereographic images by photographer or publisher and creating a catalogue of known images is a significant contribution to the field of research and will enable scholars and collectors to fit single stereographs into context or, hopefully, to note additions to this catalogue.

Like windows to another time and place, these three-dimensional images allow us an intimate glimpse of life in the past and a rare chance to see first-hand those parts of our world that have been lost through progress. In that way, they still possess the power to entertain, to educate, and to provide a remembrance just as they did when they were first made.

LEE ELLEN GRIFFITH, PH.D.
DIRECTOR
MONMOUTH COUNTY HISTORICAL ASSOCIATION

EXPLANATION

DOUBLE EXPOSURE TWO is primarily concerned with the first fifty years of stereographic photography as it relates to the history of Monmouth County, New Jersey, and other parts of the Jersey Shore.

All the daguerreotypes, ambrotypes, cartes-de-visite, tintypes and stereographs appearing in DOUBLE EXPOSURE TWO have been reproduced in their original size and condition. No attempt has been made to enlarge, reduce, crop, or retouch a single image. Rather, it has been a prime consideration, for historical accuracy, to reproduce all the photographs as they are. The images have been dated as accurately as possible.

Far from being a part of the past, stereographic photography is very much a part of these modern times. It plays a significant role in numerous educational, scientific, technological and military fields and it still remains a source of entertainment.

5 x 7 Korona Stereo Camera   ca. 1892

PREFACE

A photograph is a mirror of a moment.

In little more than one hundred and seventy-five years the camera has recorded more of mankind's poignant, tragic, dramatic and just plain day to day existence—than all the written words since the creation of the alphabet. The photograph has long been accepted as a primary reference source. The importance of the specialized field of stereographic (three-dimensional) photography, although neglected through the years, is now recognized as a major source of historical significance. This is particularly true at the local history level where stereographic photographs are frequently the only existing pictorial record of certain places or events.

DOUBLE EXPOSURE TWO is concerned with one small yet singularly important subject: the early stereographic views of Monmouth County, New Jersey. A short and very general introduction to the pioneer development of photography is necessarily included for two reasons. First to indicate stereography's proper place within the photographic field and second to recognize and understand the conditions under which photographers worked in the formative years of the industry. Looking back at that period it is apparent their one major asset was a prodigious amount of talent plus some modest photographic equipment.

The historical and social importance of the works of early photographers is now fully recognized. Once again, there is a genuine appreciation for the technical skill and a sincere admiration for the artistic ability of these cameramen who, by virtue of what they have accomplished, are historians in their own right.

The history of photography is a fascinating story. The subject has been covered by many outstanding authorities including Beaumont Newhall, Helmut and Alison Gernsheim, Robert Taft, William Culp Darrah and Floyd and Marion Rinhart.

The 1971 edition of DOUBLE EXPOSURE was the first publication to specifically document the subject of stereographic views of Monmouth County, New Jersey.

As an archivist and picture historian, I have continued to search for additional examples and information. The successful results of these last twenty-four years are significant enough to warrant publishing this new edition. DOUBLE EXPOSURE TWO is a further contribution to a continuing major project: the preservation of the pictorial history of Monmouth County and the Jersey Shore.

The first half of the book — the early history of photography — has a few changes. It is the latter half — *At a Local Level* — that has been updated and greatly expanded. The checklist of known photographers and publishers of Monmouth County stereographs has more than tripled. In addition, an initial attempt has been made to list a few of the many photographers and publishers of stereographs of the southern portion of the Jersey Coast. As a result, DOUBLE EXPOSURE TWO is a unique reference book documenting a particular facet of the photographic history of the Jersey Shore from Keyport to Cape May.

While this book represents a total of almost thirty-five years of research, the future will continue to reveal the names of additional producers of early stereographic views of the Jersey Shore. Their efforts, too, should be noted and preserved. I welcome any additions or corrections to the pages that follow.

From the beginning of this project many individuals have been extremely helpful. I am indebted to the late Professor William C. Darrah, who graciously shared precious time and invaluable knowledge; to the late Beaumont Newhall for his written comments and encouragement and, to his very end, the late Fred G. Lightfoot, whose dependable expertise helped smooth the way.

To Ronald D. Lowden Jr., a friend of many years, for his suggestions and continued interest — and to A. Verner Conover, another friend whose impressive New Jersey collection added depth to this book and eventually became part of the Moss Archives, I can only say — thank you.

I am indebted to James D. Lindemuth for sharing Ocean Grove information and to Randall Gabrielan for his timely research. With special thanks I acknowledge Karen L. Schnitzspahn for her editorial correctness.

Finally, my grateful appreciation is extended to Dr. Lee Ellen Griffith, Director, Monmouth County Historical Association, for generously consenting to write the foreword to this new edition.

GEORGE H. MOSS JR.
RUMSON, NEW JERSEY, 1995

BACKGROUND

Pioneer photographers were artists at heart.

With more than a basic understanding of light and shadow, a number of the experimenters and photographic innovators of the 1840-1860 period actually were artists who found in photography a fantastic new medium and art form that rivalled nature herself.

Perhaps more important than an artistic background was the pioneer photographer's ability to cope with the complicated chemistry of photography. This was decades before Mr. Eastman's philosophy of "you push the button – we do the rest."

In this new era of experimentation and improvisation the photographic darkroom was a laboratory to gladden the heart of the most aspiring alchemist of the Middle Ages…a little egg albumen here…a melted golden sovereign there…a pinch of sugar…a few drops of rain water…these were not incantations whispered over a witches' cauldron, but the basic raw chemicals referred to in photographic manuals as late as 1883.

Cameras were relatively simple by today's standards: no meters, filters or split second shutters and only one film speed…slow! Just the bare essentials necessary to record a moment in time. In those uncluttered days it was indeed the photographer who took the picture – not the camera. These individuals behind the lens exercised their creative and artistic talents to produce remarkable photographs of often matchless beauty.

As the late Beaumont Newhall, the distinguished Director of George Eastman House in Rochester, N.Y., pointed out - there is no single inventor of photography. Decades of experimentation by many scientifically minded individuals intent on discovering the secret of preserving that moment in time culminated in 1827 when Nicephore Niépce successfully produced the first photograph...on pewter.

Subsequent correspondence between Niépce and the co-inventor of the Diorama, Louis Jacques Mande Daguerre, ultimately led to a partnership which was terminated within four years (1833) by Niépce's sudden death. Continued experimentation by Daguerre led to a photographic process that was to profoundly effect the arts, sciences, even the very history of mankind. First presented to the public in 1839, the photographic image so clearly captured on a silvered copper plate was called a Daguerreotype.

The following paragraph, from C. Wingate's article "Light and Daguerreotype," is a simple and basic description of daguerreotype production. It appeared in the 1852 edition of the *Ladies' Keepsake and Home Library*.

> As many of our readers may not be familiar with the process by which Daguerreotypes are produced, a brief description of it may be interesting: The first thing to be done is to prepare a plate, composed of copper, faced with a thin coating of pure silver, and polished with the greatest possible care. On the accuracy with which this is done depends the whole thing. The plate is then exposed to the vapor of iodine, and placed in the camera, a box containing a large convex lens, by which the light is condensed, and brought to a focus on a screen placed behind it. Having remained in the camera from ten seconds to a minute, or more, according to the brightness of the day, the plate is removed, and exposed to the action of the vapor of mercury, by which the image formed on the silver is developed. In this state of the process the plate has a dark, purple color, and the picture is readily destroyed by the light. The grand difficulty to be remedied, and for which Daguerre labored so long, is to fix the image produced by the camera, and render it proof against the action of light. This is accomplished by washing the plate in a solution of the hypo-sulphate of soda, by which the iodine is expelled, and, finally, heating it in a bath of the chloride of gold, by which a thin transparent coating of gold is spread over the entire plate, and all change from the effects of light entirely prevented.

Portrait of a young couple. 1854
Daguerreotype by Jeremiah Gurney, New York City.
Half plate.

The Daguerreotype

The daguerreotype, considered by some to be the most beautiful image produced with a camera, is a most remarkable photograph. Some of the finest examples are to be found in Beaumont Newhall's comprehensive book published by New York Graphic Society in 1968 entitled THE DAGUERREOTYPE IN AMERICA. Daguerreotypes were made in a half dozen standard sizes ranging from the whole plate (6 1/2 x 8 1/2 in.) to a sixteenth plate (1 3/8 x 1 5/8 in.). Larger sizes which measured up to 15 x 17 inches were produced on rare occasions and were called "mammoth plates." Daguerreotypes were usually mounted in elegant leather covered cases. In the mid-1850's the thermoplastic case was introduced. Strikingly beautiful, the finest cases are more often sought after than the daguerreotypes they protect.

Man holding book. (Eyes tinted blue.)   1846
Daguerreotype by Aug. H. Morand,
New York City. Sixth plate.

Three children —   1853
one holding an orange.
Daguerreotypist unknown.
Sixth plate.

An example of a Littlefield,   1858
Parsons & Co. thermoplastic
"Union Case" depicting one of their
many popular cover designs.
4 x 5 inches (for a quarter plate).

LITTLEFIELD, PARSONS & CO.,
— MANUFACTURERS OF —
Daguerreotype Cases.

L., P. & CO.,
Are the sole Proprietors and **only**
legal Manufacturers of
UNION CASES,
WITH THE
Embracing Riveted Hinge.

Patented,
Oct. 14, 1856, & *April* 21, 1857.

The Littlefield, Parsons & Co.   1858
label which is usually found
pasted inside the "Union Case"
behind the mounted daguerreotype.

Seated man and woman holding hands. 1850
Daguerreotype by Perkins. Quarter plate.

Woman with necklace. 1853
Daguerreotype by Rufus Anson,
New York City. Ninth plate.

Portrait of a gentleman. 1854
Daguerreotype by
Edward H. Stokes,
Trenton, N. J. Sixth plate.

Two brothers. 1854
Daguerreotypist unknown.
Sixth plate.

This, one of the first published American references to the daguerreotype appeared in a New York magazine, THE KNICKERBOCKER, in December of 1839.

THE 'DAGUERREOTYPE.' — We have seen the views taken in Paris by the 'DAGUERREOTYPE,' and have no hesitation in avowing, that they are the most remarkable objects of curiosity and admiration, in the arts, that we ever beheld. Their exquisite perfection almost transcends the bounds of sober belief. Let us endeavor to convey to the reader an impression of their character. Let him suppose himself standing in the middle of Broadway, with a looking-glass held perpendicularly in his hand, in which is reflected the street, with all that therein is, for two or three miles, taking in the haziest distance. Then let him take the glass into the house, and find the impression of the entire view, in the softest light and shade, vividly retained upon its surface. This is the DAGUERREOTYPE! The views themselves are from the most interesting points of the French metropolis. We shall speak of several of them at random, as the impression of each arises in the mind, and not in the order in which they stand in the exhibition. Take, first, the Vue du Pont Notre Dame, and Palais du Justice. Mark the minute light and shade; the *perfect* clearness of every object; the extreme softness of the distance. Observe the dim, hazy aspect of the picture representing the towers of Notre Dame, with Saint Jacques la Boucherie in the distance. It was taken in a violent storm of rain; and how admirably is even *that* feature of the view preserved in the *tout ensemble*! Look, again, at the view of the Statue of Henry the Fourth and the Tuilleries, the Pont des Arts, Pont du Carousel, Pont Royal, and the Heights of Chaillot in the distance. There is not a shadow in the whole, that is not *nature itself*; there is not an object, even the most minute, embraced in that wide scope, which was not in the original; and it is impossible that one should have been omitted. Think of that! So, too, of the Tuilleries, the Champs Elysées, the Quay de la Morgue — in short, of all and every view in the whole superb collection. The shade of a shadow is frequently reflected in the river, and the very trees are taken with the *shimmer* created by the breeze, imaged in the water! Look where you will, Paris itself is before you. Here, by the silent statue of the great Henry, how often has Despair come at midnight, to plunge into eternity! By the Quay de la Morgue, remark the array of washing-boats, and the 'Ladies of the Suds' hanging out their clothes, which *almost* wave in the breeze. It was but a little below this point, that our entertaining 'American in Paris,' doubtful of the purity of the Seine water, bought a filter of charcoal, 'to intercept the petticoats, and other such articles,' as he might previously have swallowed. *There is a view, now,* which Mr. IRVING has helped to render famous. It was across that very Pont Neuf, if we have not forgotten the story, one awful night in the tempestuous times of the French revolution, when the lightning gleamed, and loud claps of thunder rattled through the lofty, narrow streets, that Gottfried Wolfgang supported his headless bride. It needs no VICTOR HUGO, to tell us that this is the time-honored *Notre Dame de Paris*. Take the view into the strongest sunlight, by the window, and survey with a glass its minutest beauties. There is not a stone traced there, that has not its archetype in the edifice. Those square towers, those Gothic arches and buttresses; the rich tracery, and that enterprising tourist looking down upon Paris — there they *were*, and here they *are*! Look sharp, and far within, you may see the very bells. What an association! What tales have the bells of Notre Dame told to Paris and the Parisians, since Pope Alexander laid her corner stone! One cannot but feel, while gazing at this scene, as did an eloquent American on first encountering similar associations: 'Something strong and stately, like the slow and majestic march of a mighty whirlwind, sweeps around those eternal towers: the mighty processions of kings, consuls, emperors, and empires, have passed over that sublime theatre.' How those bells pealed, when Napoleon's sounding bulletins came in from Italy and Germany, from Egypt and Russia! How, more recently, they clamored at midnight, when the tocsin of revolt streamed upon the hoary towers, and the tri-color floated triumphant from their summits! But leaving the times that *were*, let us come down to the days that *are*. Near where you see that hopeful member of the *sans culottides* tribe musing on the bridge, is the spot where the renowned Mrs. RAMSBOTTOM saw, for the first time, the 'statute of Henry Carter,' (Henri Quatre,) and marvelled 'whether he could be any relation to the CARTERS of Portsmouth.' The very *affiches* then 'black-guarded against the walls,' are still here. Close at hand, too, in another frame, are the 'Tooleries' and 'Penny Royal,' which so greatly delighted the old lady and her daughter Lavinia.

We have little room to speak of the 'interior' views. We can only say, in passing, that they are *perfect*. Busts, statues, curtains, pictures, are copied to the very life; and portraits are included, without the *possibility* of an incorrect likeness. Indeed, the DAGUERREOTYPE will never do for portrait painting. Its pictures are quite *too* natural, to please any other than very beautiful sitters. It has not the slightest knack at 'fancy-work.' MATTHEWS used to sing, in his 'Trip to Paris':

'Mrs. Grill is very ill!
Nothing can improve her,
Until she sees the 'Tooleries,'
And waddles through the Louvre,'

This was truthful satire, in the great mime's day; but illness, with sea-voyage cures, must decline now; for who would throw up their business and their dinners, on a voyage to see Paris or London, when one can sit in an apartment in New-York, and look at the streets, the architectural wonders, and the busy life of each crowded metropolis? We recognized, without doubt, many Frenchmen of whom we had before heard. We distinctly saw, we are confident, in the door of a restaurant, in a white apron, with sleeves rolled up, the identical cook who brought our esteemed correspondent, SANDERSON, the tough '*bifstek de mouton*,' which the latter offered him five francs to eat, but which the functionary, after turning the matter over in his mind, reluctantly declined, on the ground that 'he had an aged mother, and another relation, dependent upon his exertions!' . . . M. GOURAUD, the accomplished and gentlemanly proprietor of the 'DAGUERREOTYPE' and the only legitimate specimens of the art in this country, favored us with an examination of one or two views, which were accidentally injured in the process of being taken. But although imperfect, they were still wonderful in the general effect. The 'darkness visible,' the floods of light, the immensity of the space, and the far perspective, in their dim, obscure state, all reminded us of the English MARTIN. But our article is already too much extended; and we close by saying to all our metropolitan readers, 'Go and see the views taken by the DAGUERREOTYPE; and when M. GOURAUD commences his lectures upon the art, fail not to hear him!

Photography preserved man's image for posterity a lot quicker than the most accomplished artist could with canvas and brush. The advertisements in the column below are from the "N. Y. Sunday Mercury" advertisements of 1850.

The Plumbe National Daguerrian Gallery,
251 Broadway, upper corner of Murray street.
Instituted in 1840.
TWO PATENTS GRANTED UNDER THE GREAT SEAL OF THE UNITED STATES.
AWARDED the GOLD and SILVER MEDALS, FOUR FIRST PREMIUMS, and TWO HIGHEST HONORS, at the NATIONAL, the MASSACHUSETTS, the NEW YORK, and the PENNSYLVANIA EXHIBITIONS, respectively, for the MOST SPLENDID COLORED DAGUERREOTYPES AND BEST APPARATUS.
Portraits taken in any weather, in exquisite style.
Apparatus and stock, wholesale and retail.
Instruction given in the art.   n18 3m

LATEST FROM THE PACIFIC.
J. GURNEY, having returned from California, will be happy to see his friends and the public generally at his old-established DAGUERRIAN GALLERY, 189 BROADWAY, and will pay personal attention to all who may be desirous of procuring a perfect picture.
A Daguerreotype view of the city and harbor of San Francisco can be seen at the rooms.   d9 3m

THE LATEST IMPROVEMENTS IN
Daguerreotyping
at GURNEY'S, 189 BROADWAY—the oldest establishment of the kind in the city.
In addition to the beautiful chemical effect of his pictures, he has been opening a large skylight for taking groups or children in the shortest time possible, and with ease to the sitter. No expense has been spared in procuring the best cameras that are manufactured, and as the best materials only are used, he is prepared to take likenesses that are unsurpassed for boldness, truthfulness, beauty of finish, or durability.
Gurney attends personally to his sitters, and no picture is allowed to leave the establishment unless satisfactory to the purchaser.
Ladies and gentlemen are respectfully invited to visit the gallery.
N B—A Daguerreotype View of the City and Harbor of San Francisco can be seen at the rooms.   mh3 3m

Good Daguerreotypes
TAKEN AND ENCLOSED IN MOROCCO CASES for 50 cents each, at THOMPSON'S GALLERY, 315 BROADWAY, first door below the Hospital. Children of all ages taken in from one to five seconds, by an instrument made for that especial purpose. A superior assortment of Lockets, &c., on hand at low prices. Go and see and be satisfied.
mh10 6m   W. THOMPSON, 315 Broadway.

Broadway Daguerrean Gallery,
323 BROADWAY, New York,
OPPOSITE THE BROADWAY THEATRE.—Likenesses for FIFTY CENTS and upwards, with case. Having fitted up these rooms for the comfort and convenience of the public, all who wish a good, cheap and durable Likeness, will need no better guarantee than to know that we employ no half-way operators at this establishment, but give our personal attention to the making of Pictures, and use none but the best materials. Having had several years' experience in Daguerreotyping, we flatter ourselves that we can please the most fastidious. If there are any so foolish as to assert that it is all humbug to talk of making a *Likeness for Fifty Cents*, send them to us and we can convince them to the contrary. N. B.—Likenesses of Children made in from 3 to 12 seconds. Daguerreotypes inserted in Lockets, Rings, &c., at reasonable prices. Remember the number, 323 Broadway, opposite the Broadway Theatre, and first room above the City Hospital.   L. L. HARRINGTON, } Proprietors.
L. D. BUSWELL, }
Instructions given in the Art. Apparatus and Stock furnished at the lowest prices.   j 3 3m

National Miniature Gallery.—E. WHITE. (late J. R. Clark, Proprietor.) 247 Broadway, New-York, over the jewelry store of Ball, Tompkins & Black. The proprietor would respectfully inform citizens and strangers that this Gallery—containing over a thousand Daguerreotype Likenesses of our most distinguished men—is open for their inspection.
The proprietor after nearly eight years' experience in the Daguerrian Art—inventing and perfecting many of the improvements that have been made since its discovery by Daguerre, and which has brought it to its present state of perfection—has purchased the above named Gallery—and flatters himself that he will not only sustain, but increase its reputation and the acknowledged high character of the establishment.
The superior arrangements for light, and the present incomparable process, (known only at this place,) enable us to take Daguerreotype Miniatures that excel all others in their mellow and harmonious tone, yet clear and distinct in outline, and without the disagreeable hue that has hitherto been the chief objection to Daguerreotype Portraits.
To convince the most incredulous of the great superiority of Pictures taken at this place, they are respectfully invited to visit the Gallery and judge for themselves. The prices as formerly.   jy24 1meodis

The above advertisement is from the "New York Tribune," July 24, 1848.

ROOTS DAGUERREAN GALLERY.—There is no place like this in New York for perfect daguerreotypes. Here is displayed a multitude of the most beautiful specimens of this art, showing the perfection of Mr. Root's mode of taking them. This gentleman has placed in the Crystal Palace some forty or fifty pieces, which attract great attention, and will probably secure the first prize. Any one who has seen them cannot but admire the sharpness of the figure, the perfection of the drapery, and especially the remarkably clear and natural expression of the eye—one of the most difficult attainments in this art. No higher testimony can be given to the excellence of Mr. Root's daguerreotypes than the constant press of business on his hands, his rooms being thronged every day with visitors. He succeeds admirably in taking the likenesses of children. And what mother would not love to preserve the infant features of her children to look upon in after years, especially should they be taken away by death. We have rarely seen a more beautiful illustration of this than in the following:

> Sweet child, that angel face must fade,
>   As years shall come and go,
> For time doth ever mar the fair
>   And bright of all below.
> But thy fond mother's jealous care
>   Hath robbed the yawning tomb,
> And by the might of art, hath fixed
>   For e'er thy youthful bloom.
> Within her sacred shrine there hangs
>   In all its infant grace,
> On Root's unequaled, perfect plate,
>   Her darling's glorious face.
> Then, mother of the blooming child,
>   Trust not the fleeting hours,
> But, as this mother did by her's,
>   Do thou at once by yours.
> Then, should the sudden dart of death
>   Your loved one call away,
> You'd bless the hint by which you had
>   The picture done to day,
>   By ROOT, 363 Broadway.

Advertising takes many forms. This column appeared in an 1853 edition of "The Christian Parlor Magazine." Marcus A. Root and his brother Samuel operated this studio from 1849 to 1857.

Newell Family.
Daguerreotype by Clark, New Brunswick, N.J.
Whole plate.

1853
MONMOUTH COUNTY HISTORICAL ASSOCIATION

James Newell and wife Eliza, (Standing left to right) A.D. Newell, M.D., Hon. William A. Newell (Ex-Governor of New Jersey and founder of the U. S. Life Saving Service), Col. John W. Newell and W. D. Newell, M.D.

Record Office, Hightstown, N.J.　　1853
Daguerreotypist unknown.
Sixth plate.　　　　　　　　　MCHA

"Turner's Court."　　　　　　　1853
Daguerreotypist unknown.
Quarter Plate.

A daguerreotype is a mirror image. For esthetic reasons the above two daguerreotypes ("Record Office" and "Turner's Court") have been printed in reverse on this page to effect a normal appearance.

Girl with white collar.　　1850
Daguerreotypist unknown.
Sixteenth plate.

Photographic chemical bottles with original labels circa 1861.

Woman with book.
Daguerreotypist unknown.
Sixth plate.

Man with book. Case 1857
Daguerreotypist unknown.
Daguerreotypes 1852
Sixth plate.

Young woman in plaid dress. Tinted 1854
Daguerreotypist unknown.
Sixth plate.

An advertising card for A. A. Fish 1853
found on the back of a mounted
daguerreotytpe.

Woman with cap and shawl.   1854
Daguerreotype by Assay, Philadelphia, Pa.
Sixth plate.

Portrait of a young man.   1847
Daguerreotypist unknown.
Frame removed to show plate
maker's name at edge of top
right: SCOVILLS. (The Scovill
Mfg. Co. of Waterbury, Conn.)
Sixth plate.

Portrait of a young woman.   1852
Daguerreotypist unknown.
Ninth plate.

The art of taking a photograph has not changed since the first pictures were taken. Some problems that plagued the unskilled operator in this

430　　　　　　　　　HARPER'S NEW MONTHLY MAGAZINE.

Ninth Trial.—Pretty Girl over the Way throws a light on Stubbs's nose with Mirror.

Tenth Trial.—Stubbs sees Pretty Girl over the Way, and nods at her.

Eleventh Trial.—Stubbs turns to look at Pretty Girl, but recovers his position.

Twelfth Trial.—Pretty Girl smiles at Stubbs. He chuckles, and moves his Head.

Thirteenth Trial.—Stubbs arranges his Cravat to Captivate Pretty Girl.

Fourteenth Trial.—Pretty Girl goes away. Stubbs begins to grow tired, and Yawns.

Fifteenth Trial.—Boy forgets, and lets Stubbs sit Ten Minutes.

Sixteenth Trial.—JONES, the Great Operator, returns, and takes Stubbs's Picture at once.

cartoon are often a problem today. The cartoon appeared in the 1856, volume XIII, edition of HARPER'S NEW MONTHLY MAGAZINE.

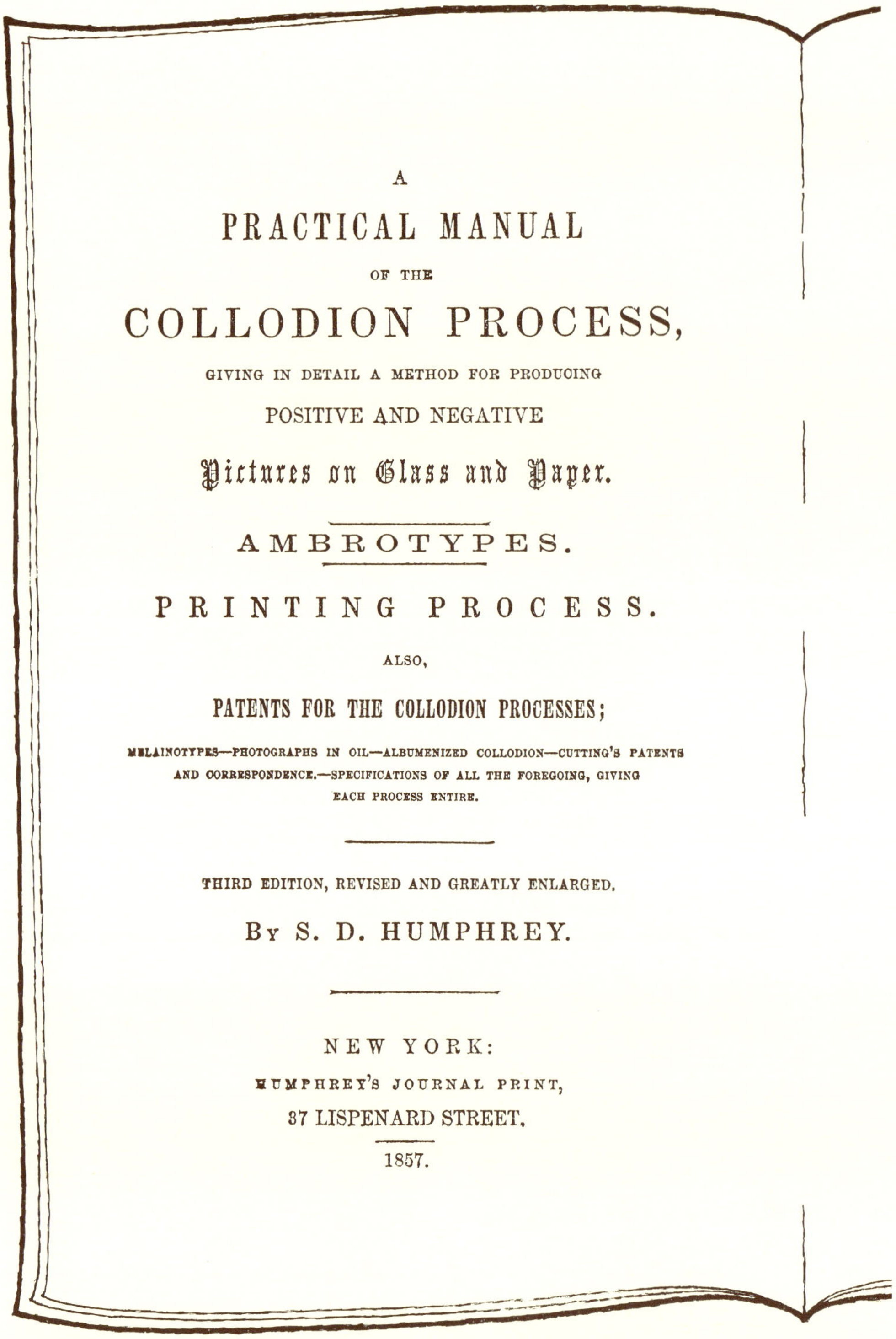

A
PRACTICAL MANUAL
OF THE
COLLODION PROCESS,

GIVING IN DETAIL A METHOD FOR PRODUCING

POSITIVE AND NEGATIVE

Pictures on Glass and Paper.

AMBROTYPES.

PRINTING PROCESS.

ALSO,

PATENTS FOR THE COLLODION PROCESSES;

MELAINOTYPES—PHOTOGRAPHS IN OIL—ALBUMENIZED COLLODION—CUTTING'S PATENTS
AND CORRESPONDENCE.—SPECIFICATIONS OF ALL THE FOREGOING, GIVING
EACH PROCESS ENTIRE.

THIRD EDITION, REVISED AND GREATLY ENLARGED.

By S. D. HUMPHREY.

NEW YORK:
HUMPHREY'S JOURNAL PRINT,
37 LISPENARD STREET.
1857.

"Humphrey's Manual," reproduced in part on the next seven pages, graphically presents the technical world of the pioneer photographer.

CHAPTER II.

CAMERA—ARRANGEMENT OF LENSES—CAMERA TUBES—CAMERA-BOXES, BELLOWS, AND COPYING—CAMERA STANDS—HEAD RESTS—CLEANING VICE—NITRATE BATH—LEVELING STANDS—PRINTING FRAMES—COLLODION VIALS.

BABTISTA PORTA, when he saw for the first time, on the walls of his dark chamber, the images of external nature, pictured by a sunbeam which found its way through only a small hole, little thought of the importance which would be attached to the instrument he was, from this cause, led to invent. The camera obscura of this Italian philosopher remained as a mere scientific toy for years, and it was not until Daguerre's discovery that its true value was estimated. It now plays a very important part in giving employment to at least *ten thousand* persons in this country alone.

It is of the utmost importance, in selecting a set of apparatus, to secure a good camera; for without such no one can obtain fine pictures. In testing it, see that it gives the pupil of the eye and lineaments of the features sharp and distinct; and that the whole image on the ground glass has a fine pearly hue. Look also to the field, and observe that the focus is good at the centre and extreme edges of the ground glass at the same time. A poor camera generally gives a misty image, with the lights and shades apparently running together. The best American cameras are fully equal to those imported, while they cost much less; but there are great numbers sold which are not worth using.

If a lens gives a well defined image on the ground glass, it should do the same on the plate. Many a valuable lens has been condemned for failing in this, merely in consequence of the plate-holder not being in focus with the ground-glass. In case of deficiency in this, put a glass into the holder, lay a rule across the face, and measure the distance between them very exactly; measure the ground-glass in the same way, and make the distance agree perfectly, by moving the ground-glass either back or forward in the frame, as the case may be, so that the surface of the glass plate shall occupy precisely the same position as the face of the ground-glass when in the camera.

It is very desirable that the operator should understand the arrangement of the lenses in the tube; it not unfrequently happens, that in taking out the "glasses" to clean them, he does not return them to their proper places, and the result is that his "camera is spoiled." A couple of illustrations and a few remarks will be sufficient to enable any one to replace the lenses in them properly. Fig. 13

Fig. 13.

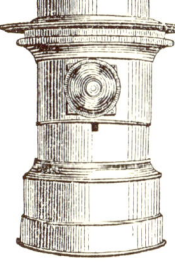
Fig. 14

represents the tube for holding the lens, and Fig. 14 shows their arrangement. It will be seen that the two

POSITION OF LENSES IN THE TUBE.

back lenses have a small space between them; this separation is kept by a small tube or ring of the same circumference as the lens. The two front lenses are nearest together. It will be observed that the two thick lenses are towards each other; these are made of *flint glass* containing much oxide of lead. The other two are double convex, and are made of *crown glass*. By noting the fact that the two cemented lenses go in the front of the tube, the glass having the thickest edge goes inside, and that the *thickest lens* of the other two goes in first, from the back of the tube, it will not be easy for the operator to make a mistake in returning the "glasses."

"I will remark that a diaphragm diminishes both chromatic and spherical aberration, by cutting off the outside portion of the lens. It lessens the brilliancy of the image, but improves the distinctness by preventing various rays from interfering with and confusing each other; it also causes a variety of objects at different distances to be in focus at the same time."

The tube containing the lenses is to be mounted on a box (camera-box) as in Fig. 15. For this purpose there are

Fig. 15.

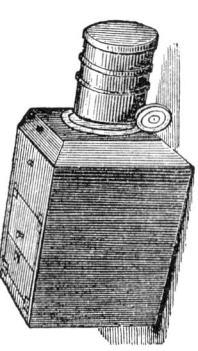

several patterns of boxes, from among which I have made

CAMERA BOXES.

two selections of the most approved, and represent them by cuts, Figs. 16, 17, 18. [Fig. 16.]

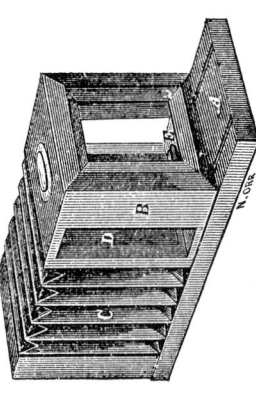

Figs. 16 and 17 represent a bellows-box which is probably more in use than all the other patterns together. They serve both for copying and taking portraits from life. A is

Fig. 17.

the base; B is the back and *sliding*-box; C, bellows, which admits of extension or contraction; D is the opening to receive the carriage A, Fig. 17; E is a thumb screw to hold the sliding-box at any required distance. Fig. 17 represents the plate-holder and ground glass frame.

A, carriage to pass through D, Fig. 16; B, frame for ground-glass, which may be turned in a horizontal or perpendicular position; C, a movable plate-holder held in place by means of springs; D, reducing holder, with bottom and plate to hold the glass plate: any size of reducing frame can be put in frame C; E E, spring bottom to keep frame

CAMERA BOXES.

D in place; F, slide; G, thumb-screw, when the carriage is to be put in or taken out of the box, Fig 16; H H, spring bottom to hold B in place.

Bellows-boxes can be obtained which receive the plate-holder from the top, the same as in the copying-box, Figs. 15 and 18. The common wood, or "copying-box," is represented by Fig. 18.

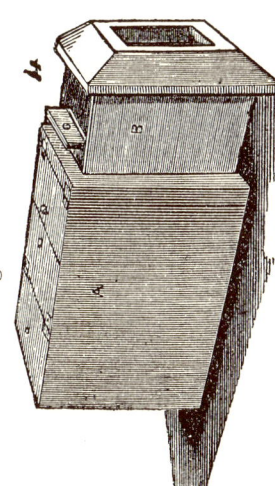

Fig 18.

A, being the main or outside box, is made of wood veneered with rosewood; B is another box which fits into A, sliding in and out as required. The ground glass and plate-holders fit grooves made in the inside box.

In regard to plate-holders or tablets for holding the glass plates, it need only be said that the camera-boxes are accompanied with a complete set, so arranged that the light is wholly excluded from the plate while drawing out or pushing in the slide, for shutting off the light while the holder is out of the box. Should any one be desirous of using the same camera, for taking both glass and daguerreotype pictures, it will be necessary for him to be provided with two sets of tablets for his box, one for each process.

CAMERA STANDS.

There are several patterns of these; almost every dealer has some particular style, which, if not for beauty, for his interest, suits his purposes best. Among the assortment, I will present only two illustrations. The first, Fig. 19, represents one which has an advantage over many others; it is made of cast iron, and of an ornamental pattern:—A, base on castors; B, fluted hollow column, which admits the iron tube C, which has on one side a hollow tooth rack to receive a spiral thread on the inner face of wheel D; this wheel, when turned, elevates or lowers the

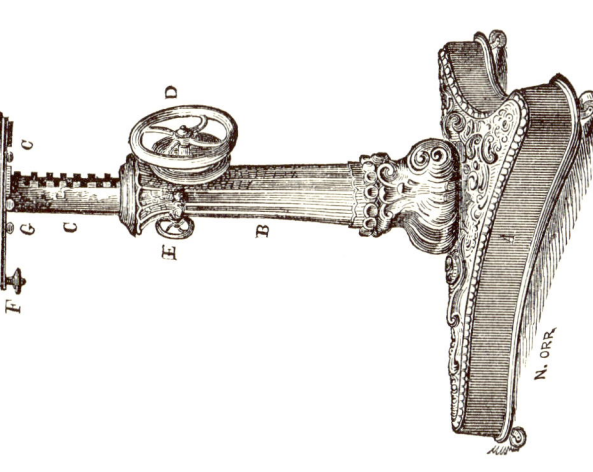

Fig. 19.

CAMERA STANDS, ARM STANDS.

tube C to any desired height; E, thumb wheel attached to a screw which sets against tube C, to hold it in position, F, a pinion by which the camera can be directed; G G, thumb screws to hold the two plates together when in position. It is quite heavy, stands *firm and solid*, and is not liable to be moved by the jar from walking over the floor. For permanently located operators these are the most desirable; but for those who are moving about from place to place, and those who wish to take views, a

Fig. 21.

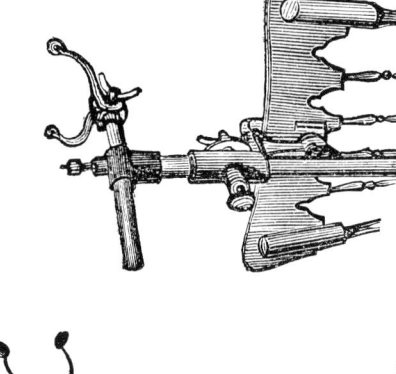

Fig. 20.

lighter article would be more convenient, such as one represented at Fig. 20. This stand is made principally of wood, and can be readily taken apart, so as to be packed in an ordinary sized trunk.

Fig. 21 represents a small "Jenny Lind stand," and is

HEAD RESTS.

a very convenient article for the sitter to lean a hand or arm upon while sitting for a portrait. It is fixed with a rod for raising or lowering the top, and can be adjusted to any required height.

HEAD RESTS.

There are several patterns of head supports, or, as they are commonly called, head rests, in use by the profession. I give two illustrations (Figs. 22 and 23). The

Fig. 22. Fig. 23.

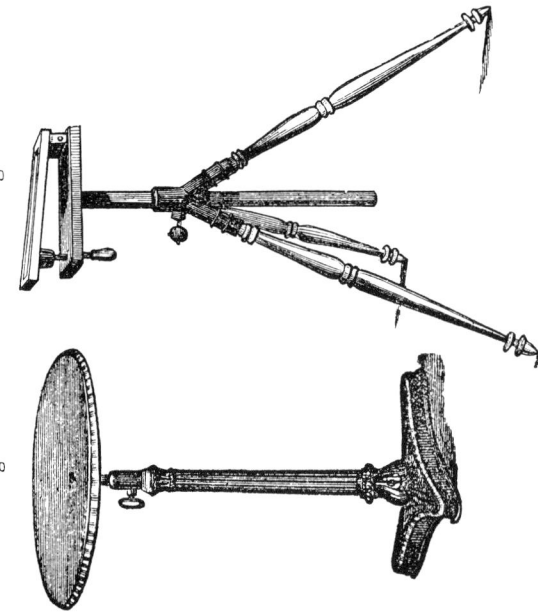

first is an independent iron rest, known as the "Jenny Lind Rest," and the other is for fastening to the back of a chair, as seen in the cut. For general use, I would recommend the iron independent rest as far more advisable than any other.

VICES FOR HOLDING GLASS.

The article used for holding the glass, during the process of cleaning, is called a vice; and, of the numerous

PLATE-HOLDERS, BATH, DIPPING RODS.

styles recently introduced, I find none that I would prefer to the old one known in market as "Peck's Vice;" it is simple and easy in operation, and at the same time is effectual. Fig. 24 represents this vice, which is to be

Fig. 24.

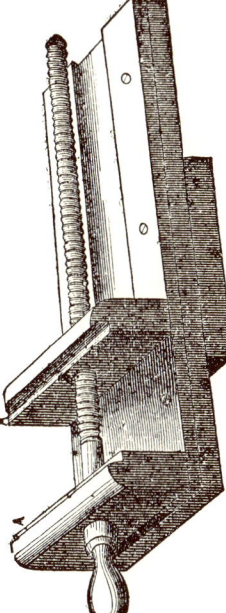

firmly secured to a bench; the small piece of wood attached to the bottom is of no use. A A are the grooves for receiving the daguerreotype plate-block; but as they are too deep for the glass, I pin on a small strip of wood, so that the upper edge of the glass will be a little above the projection of the vice.

NITRATE BATHS AND DIPPING RODS.

The accompanying illustration, Fig. 25, *a*, represents a

Fig. 25.　　Fig. 26.　Fig. 27.

　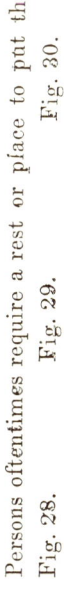

bath for holding the nitrate of silver solution. This

LEVELING STANDS.

shape is of my own suggestion, and the best adapted to the wants of the photographer. It will be seen that the front side is rounding, with a curve extending from side to side. By this shape, the *face* of the glass is protected from coming in contact with the side of the bath—both edges of it turning so as to prevent injury. There is a small projection on the top, at the opposite side of the oval; this is to allow the solution to flow over and wash off any dust that may have gathered upon the surface of the solution. This wash runs out of a small tube, as is shown in the cut. Any convenient vessel can be placed under it to receive the liquid. This can be filtered and returned as often as required. I am not in the practice of filling my baths full of solution, but always keep them filtered and clean; hence saving an excess of solution.

b represents a little support, which is secured at its base upon the shelf, to hold the bath in a slightly inclined position, which is preferable to having it stand perpendicularly.

LEVELING STANDS.

Persons oftentimes require a rest or place to put their

Fig. 28.　　Fig. 29.　　　Fig. 30.

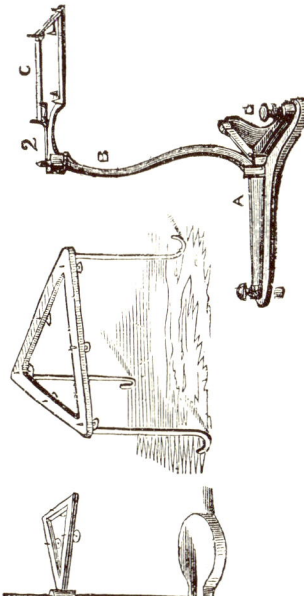

glass during development or washing the picture. Either

of the stands represented by the annexed cut will answer the purpose.

Fig. 30 is known to the daguerreotype operator as a "gilding stand," and is the one best adapted to the wants of operators on glass. It may be so arranged as to give the surface of the glass a water-level; D D are thumb-screws, by means of which, when properly regulated, the frame C may hold glass perfectly level and a large quantity of solution may be poured over the surface.

PRINTING FRAMES.

There are numerous methods and apparatus used for holding the negative and the paper during exposure to the light. The following illustrations represent a convenient and economical frame for this purpose.

Fig. 31.   Fig. 32.

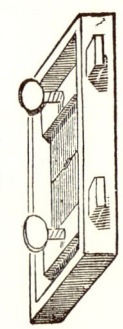

Fig. 31 represents the front of the frame. The negative glass is held upon it by springs attached by screws to the bottom half of the frame, A, so that they can be turned on or off, to suit the different sizes of glass. On the other end of the spring are wooden buttons, which are placed on the edges of the glass negative, holding it in its place, and pressing it firmly against the paper which is placed under it. This frame is made of two pieces of inch board, which are connected by hinges, falling over

as seen in Fig. 32, B being the half that is movable. This movable half is secured in position by means of a wooden button, attached to A on the back and under B, as seen in Fig. 32. The separate pieces, A and B, are bevelled where they connect, as seen by Fig. 31. D (in Fig. 32) is one of the springs, which can be seen in Fig. 31.

The entire bed or face of the frame, A and B, should be covered with a thick piece of satinet cloth, which may be pasted to the lower half, A, and extended over the entire surface of A and B. This forms a pad for the paper.

This printing frame can be easily made by any cabinet-maker or carpenter. The springs may be of sheet iron or brass—either will be found sufficiently stiff for the purpose. Every operator should be provided with from four to ten frames: the saving of time will be found to amply repay the expenditure necessary for a good supply.

Another article called a pressure frame, is represented in the accompanying figure. This is more expensive than the first, and is by some considered preferable.

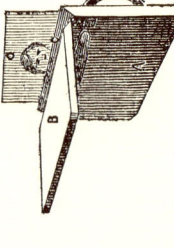

Fig. 33.

Another cheap, convenient and equally good arrangement for holding the negative and paper, is to take three glasses—say one a full size, being the one having the negative upon it; and then take two glasses, each just half the size of the negative, and have a piece of *very thick heavy* cloth cut the size of the negative glass, which can be put between it and the two half glasses, and then they can be held together by means of the common spring clothes pin.

COLLODION VIALS.—COLOR BOXES.

The advantage of the two glasses at the back is, that one can be entirely removed while the picture is being examined, and afterwards returned without, in the least, moving the impression.

Collodion Vial.—Color Boxes.

This shaped vial is made expressly for collodion, to which purpose it is admirably adapted. It has a wide

Fig. 34.   Fig. 35.

 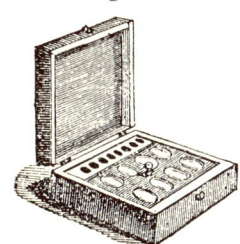

mouth, and is so constructed that the liquid flows clear and free. It is deep, and with a heavy protruding base, to prevent its falling. There are two sizes made at present, one to contain $2\frac{1}{2}$ ounces—the other, $1\frac{1}{2}$ ounce. I generally use the smaller ones, but always keep on hand, and would not be without, a few of the larger size.

Fig. 35 represents a color-box. These can be had of any dealer, completely fitted, with color and brushes for use.

Crude experiments with photographic processes on paper were undertaken as early as 1836. In 1841, English scientist William Henry Fox Talbot produced a particularly successful paper process called the Talbotype. The daguerreotype was an original positive picture which could not be readily duplicated as there was no negative. Talbot's process produced a paper negative first from which any number of duplicate positive pictures could be made.

Glass had been used in rudimentary photographic experiments in 1822 by Niépce, but it was not until 1848 that a feasible method was perfected. The "albumen-on-glass" process involved coating photographic plates with egg white and other chemicals. The resulting ability to capture fine detail was particularly suited for positive glass pictures i.e. magic lantern slides and early glass stereographic views. These sensitized ambrotype plates could be kept a few days before exposure whereas the original daguerreotype plates could only be prepared just prior to exposure.

The Ambrotype

A tremendous leap forward in the science of photography took place in 1851 with the introduction of the wet collodion process, a singular contribution of English sculptor Frederick Scott Archer. By applying collodion and other chemicals to glass, this new process shortened by eighty per cent the exposure time of sensitized photographic glass plates. One disadvantage was that chemical operations had to be completed immediately: once coated the glass plate had to be exposed and developed right away. A bulky mobile darkroom had to accompany the cameraman. On the other hand, the tremendous advantage gained by shortened time exposures greatly outweighed the problem of cumbersome portable darkrooms in the field.

For years, time exposures of many seconds, minutes - even hours were necessary to record a photographic image. Arresting motion was a dream. With the advent of the wet collodion process and improved optics (both of which contributed to shorter time exposures) the use of simple gravity drop shutters soon enabled photographers to achieve this dream. It was called "instantaneous photography."

The result of the collodion process and combined efforts of Frederick Scott Archer and Peter Wickens Fry was the ambrotype. So named by Philadelphia daguerreotypist Marcus A. Root, this photograph on glass soon replaced the daguerreotype. Almost always found mounted in what are commonly called "daguerreotype cases," ambrotypes are easily distinguishable from earlier daguerreotypes. The ambrotype is a glass negative that achieves its positive or picture quality by being pressed against a black backing in the photographic case. The daguerreotype is a positive picture on a silvered copper plate. Easily identified because of its highly polished mirror-like surface, a daguerreotype can only be viewed when held at a certain angle.

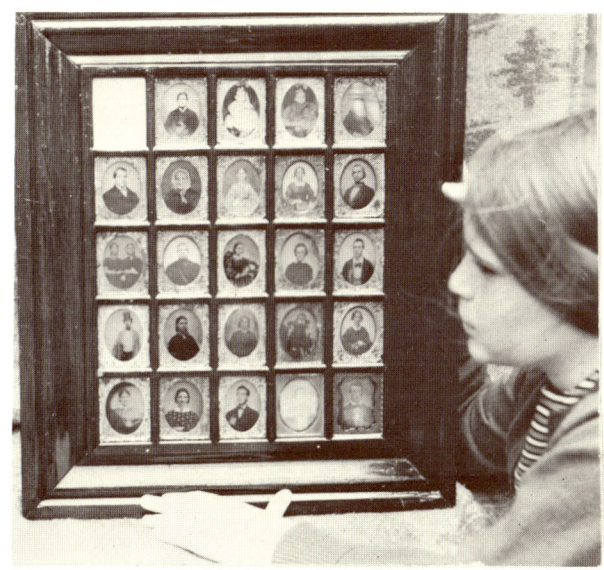

Illustrated above (in 1970) are twenty-five ambrotypes mounted in a rare studio display frame circa 1858. These frames varied in size and were used to display samples of a photographer's work.

While most ambrotypes do not compare in beauty to a finished daguerreotype, there are many notable exceptions and a good ambrotype is indeed a fine photograph. Ambrotypes were made in most of the standard daguerreotype sizes. As previously mentioned, they are found mounted in what would appear to be a daguerreotype case.

Man with beard. 1859
Ambrotype.
2 3/4 x 3 1/4 in.

Same portrait with black backing removed to show negative properties of an ambrotype.

Portrait of a father and two sons. 1858
Ambrotype.
4 1/4 x 5 1/2 in.

Woman with earrings.   1856
Ambrotype by Chace & Hawes.
2 3/4 x 3 1/4 in.

Portrait of a well-dressed   1859
young man.
Ambrotype.
2 3/4 x 3 1/4 in.

Baby in carriage.   1857
Ambrotype.
2 3/4 x 3 1/4 in.

Millie Bland.   1858
Ambrotype.
2 3/4 x 3 1/4 in.

Portrait of a seated gentleman. 1858
Ambrotype.
3 1/4 x 4 1/4 in.

Seated woman. July 26, 1858
Ambrotype.
1 3/4 x 2 3/8 in.

Man with two sisters. 1856
Ambrotype by L. G. Bean, Lowell, Mass.
2 3/4 x 3 1/4 in.

L. G. Bean's advertising card found in the ambrotype case at right.

Copy of silhouette.   1858
Ambrotype.
2 3/4 x 3 1/4 in.

Inscribed below the bust: "Cut with the mouth by M. A. Honeywell." New Hampshire born (1757), Miss Honeywell had no hands and only three toes on one foot. A prodigy, she learned to write and make silhouttes with her mouth and toes. A gifted artist in spite of her handicap, she continued using her talents until 1848. The original silhouette was probably three times the size of this unique ambrotype copy.

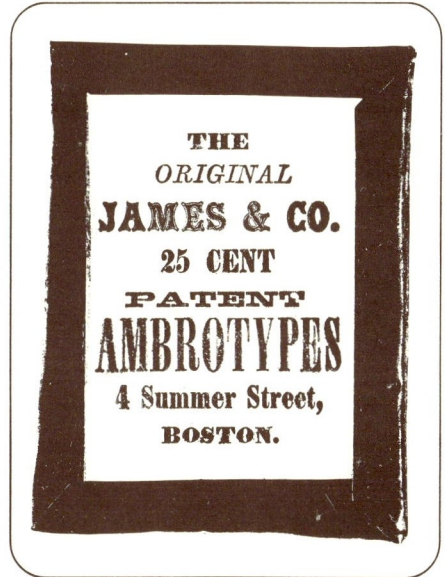

Not too commonly found, advertising cards were placed   1858
on the backs of mounted ambrotypes. The Union Art
Gallery of Taunton and James & Co.
of Boston are typical cards.

PHOTOGRAPHIC OPERATING ROOM.

The "Photographic Operating Room" was a simple but effective studio. The sun was the main source of illumination. The photographer posed his subject in front of painted scenery or a simulated fireplace and mantle. Headrests, a chair and another camera (tintype, in this illustration) complete the bare necessities.

HARPER'S NEW MONTHLY MAGAZINE. SEPTEMBER, 1869.

THE PHOTOGRAPHER'S OUTFIT.

Once outside of his studio, the pioneer photographer virtually needed a pack horse to transport all the chemicals and equipment of his trade. In spite of this cumbersome operation many beautiful and historically significant photographs were produced by these talented men in the field.

HARPER'S NEW MONTHLY MAGAZINE. SEPTEMBER, 1869.

Self portrait. 1890
J. W. Krosse, Aurora, Ill.

    A far cry from the professional 35 mm camera of today, this giant produced a glass negative 20 by 24 inches!

MY SITTERS: DIFFICULTIES OF PHOTOGRAPHY.

THE ELDERLY YOUNG LADY, IN THE JULIET POSE.

THE SITTER WHO ALWAYS FELL ASLEEP.

THE MAN WHO WANTED HIS "DORG TUK."

THE TRAGICALLY-MINDED SITTER, IN A FANCY DRESS.

THE DUTCH FAMILY, WHO WOULD ALL "GO IN ONE CART."

THE THEATRICRL JIG-DANCER, WHO, BY SHIFTING HIS POSE, GETS SEVERAL SUPERFLUOUS ARMS AND LEGS.

On April 14, 1866, Frank Leslie published this series of cartoons in the "Chimney Corner." They indicate that even the skilled cameraman often had frustrating problems...his subjects!

The Carte-de-visite

The Civil War, as Professor Robert Taft noted, greatly stimulated the photographic industry. The carte-de-visite or card photograph, was a small paper photograph mounted on a card. Measuring about two and a half by four inches in size, it was introduced into the United States just prior to the Civil War. This popular photograph was produced in such quantities that both the daguerreotype and the ambrotype soon faded into photographic history. The carte-de-visite and the tintype were to fill family albums for decades. The carte-de-visite was made until the early 1880's. At that time the dry photographic plate process was introduced. Tintypes, which will be discussed later, continued to be produced into the Twentieth Century. One interesting aspect of the carte-de-visite is that thousands of personalities of the period were photographed. Their images had mass popular appeal (not unlike baseball cards today). As a result, many fascinating collections were formed more than a century ago. Fortunate is the individual who finds an album with such a desirable collection today.

"N.J. Col. Inst., Bordentown, N.J. Dec. 1868

T. H. Rittenhouse, Boardman Gaskil, Harry T. Peace, Joshua W. Brown, Walter Satterthwait, Wm. Jud. Tenibury, Clayton Smith, Emma Steele, Eliz. Schooley, Mary Bunting, Tillie Haas, Miss Bruere, Lilla Lemley."

Mrs. Greenleaf. 1865
Photo by J. E. McClees, Artist,
Phila., Pa.

Portrait of a gentleman. 1865
Photo by Henry M. Wells,
Cambridge, N.Y.

These exceptionally fine formal portraits, evidence of outstanding artistic photographic capabilities and taken over a century and a quarter ago, rival the traditional portraits of brush and canvas.

1870

Somewhat suspiciously, three chubby children eye the cameraman. Photo by L. D. Johnson, Vineland, N. J.

The camera was among the most common symbol often found as an integral part of a photographer's logo. These imprints are from the backs of cartes-de-visite.

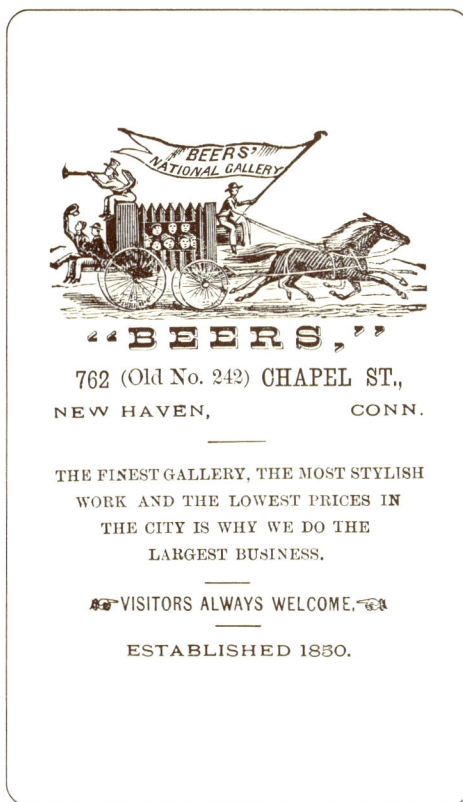

James M. French, butcher.   1873
Photo by Frank H. Price,
Elizabeth, N. J.

A delightful picture of a man who obviously took pride in his profession.

Unidentified nurse and child.   1865
Photo by S. Anderson,
New Orleans, La.

"Henry Heerdt, Aged 19 yrs.
Died May 17 1869"
Photo by A. M. Burroughs,
New York City.

Two stylish gentlemen.
A carte-de-visite copy of
a daguerreotype (ca 1853).
Photographer unknown.

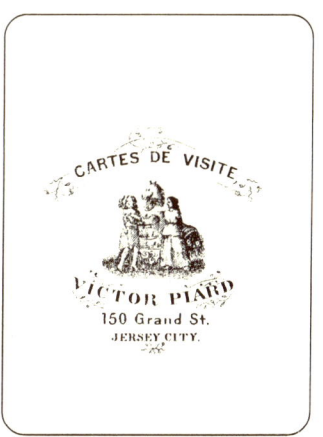

The American Eagle and the American Flag were other popular symbols, but symbols gradually gave way to design and text as photographers took advantage of the free advertising space on the back of a carte-de-visite.

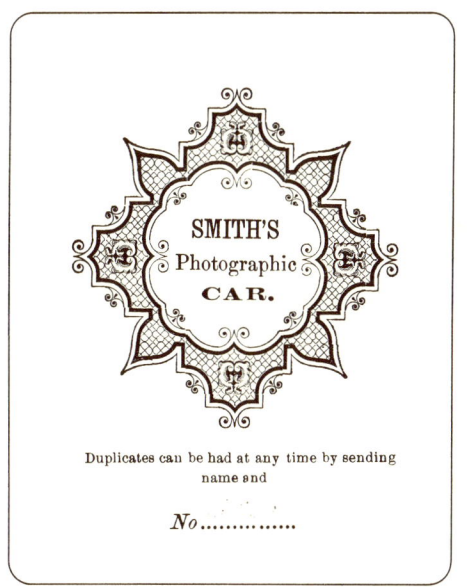
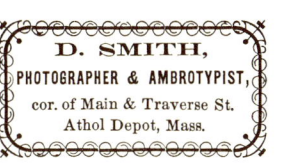

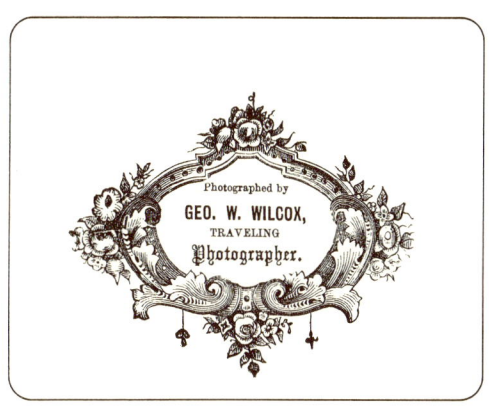

Two Civil War soldiers.   1864
Photographer unknown.

In this typical Civil War era carte-de-visite, two brothers had their picture taken for the family back home.

Portrait of a young lady.   APRIL 8, 1862.
Photo by Thompson, Norwich, Conn.

Artemus Ward.   1865
*Photo by Le Rue Lemer,
Harrisburg, Pa.*

Artemus Ward, was the pseudonym of American humorist Charles F. Browne.

Lillian Adelaide Neilson.   1877
Photo by Napoleon Sarony.

Miss Neilson, a most gifted English Shakespearean actress, made three tours in the United States. She died in France in 1880 at thirty years of age.

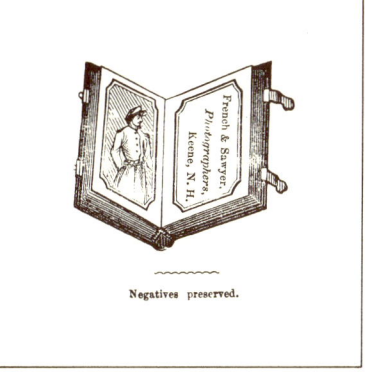

The great variety of artistic images found on the backs of most cartes-de-viste represent an interesting and revealing photography-related collection.

The carte-de-visite album was a much used prop. It appears frequently in early photographs as well as on the backs of cartes-de-visite.

1867
*Photo by James D. Powers,
Springfield, Vt.*

Studio props were either painted backdrops, a classic column or part of a hanging drape complete with tassel. The photo album completed the picture.

*Photo by L. P. Vail,
Palmyra, N. Y.*   1875

Photographer Vail also sold stereographic views and stereoscopes and included them in this particular portrait.

1869
*Photo by Burwell & Homan,
New Haven, Conn.*

The carte-de-visite album was beautifully made - usually bound in leather with intricate brass clasps. Reminiscent of a Medieval Book of Hours, its contents were no less treasured.

FROM
S. Piper's
Photographic Studio.

Pictures made **LIFE SIZE**, or any other, with our *MAMMOTH SOLAR CAMERA*, from this card or from Old Pictures, and finished in Water Colors, India Ink, or in Oil, at Piper's Studio, by a **FIRST-CLASS ARTIST**, and warranted to suit in every particular, for from $5 to $60. Shall be pleased to show you specimens at any time.

S. PIPER,
939 *Elm Street, Manchester, N. H.*

Savage and Ottinger,
SALT LAKE CITY,
Pioneer Fine Art Gallery.
—o—
Views in Utah, Idaho and Montana.
Album, Stereoscopic and larger sizes.

Mezzo-Tinto Photographs,
Process patented July 16, 1867
Meinerth's License, No. 166.

H. L. KILGORE,
PHOTOGRAPHER,
BELFAST, MAINE.

EXCLUSIVE RIGHT FOR BELFAST

E. C. HAMILL,
Photographer,
West Side Public Square.
Opposite Court House
MONMOUTH, ILL.

Photographs from Card to Life size. Ambrotypes, Gems and Oval Frames of every description.
Special attention paid to copying and enlarging Pictures.

BEAL,
Photographer,
271 Main St.,
WORCESTER.

PRICE LIST.
1 doz. . $2.50
1-2 doz. . 1.50
Duplicates.
1 doz. . 2.00
1-2 doz. . 1.00
All Negatives preserved.

1879.

J. A. French,
Photographer,
And Publisher of
Stereoscopic Views,

Additional Copies Furnished.   **KEENE, N. H.**

The thousands of photographers who produced cartes-de-visite have literally left their mark on the backs of their photographic endeavors. Each imprint, a tiny bit of history, is often the only record of a particular photographer from the distant past.

1866
*General Santa Anna.
Photo by J. Gurney & Son,
New York City.*

General and politician, Santa Anna commanded the Mexican Army against the United States in the War with Mexico (1846-48).

1863
"Commodore Nutt and Miss Minnie Warren as Groomsman & Bridesmaid."

"From a photographic negative by Brady. Published by E. & H.T. Anthony, NewYork City."

Actors, authors, statesmen, royalty and generals, all the personalities of the period, often can be found intermingled with family portraits in a carte-de-visite album.

1870
*James Fisk Jr.
Photographer unknown.*

Colonel of the Ninth Regiment of the New York Guards and partner of financier Jay Gould, "Jubilee Jim" was a frequent summer visitor to Long Branch, New Jersey.

1863
*Fannie Virginia Casseopia Lawrence.
Photo by Kellog Bros., Hartford, Conn.*

Beautiful examples of the wood engraver's art, each carte-de-visite imprint reflects the period of the 1860's and 1870's.

Union Soldier.   1864
Tintype, mounted in
Scovill Mfg. Company frame.

The Tintype

One other easily identifiable "type" of photograph is the tintype. Originally called the ferrotype, it was the contribution, in 1855, of Hamilton L. Smith, a natural science professor at Kenyon College, Gambier, Ohio. The tintype enjoyed equal popularity with the carte-de-visite. This was particularly true at military encampments during the Civil War. Itinerant cameramen worked overtime producing pictures for "the folks back home."

Generally speaking, most daguerreotypes and ambrotypes are quite formal portraits of subjects in a classic pose…the photographic artist painting with light rather than oils. The cartes-de-visite were less expensive and thus reached a broader segment of society. They are often examples of more relaxed subjects in informal poses.

However, it is the humble tintype, everyman's canvas, that captured the complete photographic range – from formal portrait to contrived gag shot. Available to all, although little more than a professional snapshot, it caused America to lose her inhibitions before a camera. Having a picture taken was fun at last!

Mr. & Mrs. David Moss. 1872
Tintype.
New York City.
A typical formal portrait of the period.

The formal pose has finally 1890
given way to the gag shot. A humorous
tintype, "Morning Service at Hillside
11 A.M." seems like it would attract
quite a following.

Tintypes or ferrotypes varied in size from the whole plate (6 1/2 x 8 1/2 in.) down to a miniature made to be mounted in a ring. The most common size was mounted in a card of about the same dimensions as a carte-de-visite. A window cut in the card framed the tintype which was mounted from the rear and held in place by a label pasted on the back. As seen by illustrations in this chapter, ferrotypists were quick to take advantage of those labels for advertising purposes.

1867
An example of one of
the smaller standard
size tintypes. Quite
attractive in the shining
metal frame, it was
half the size of the
equally popular GEM.

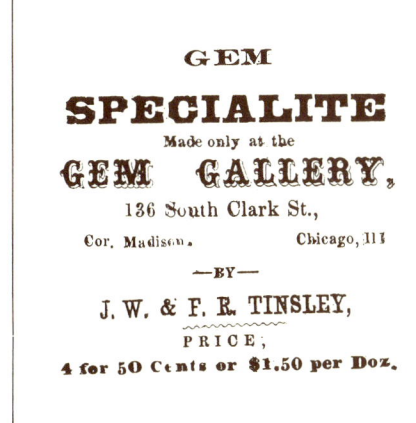 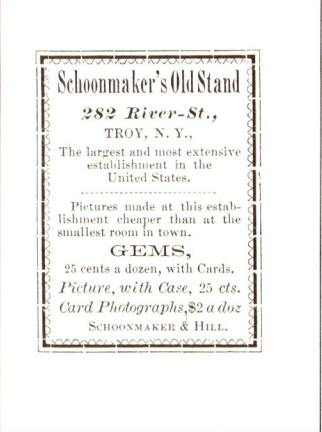

43

A delightful portrait of what just might be a group of Shaker women. Tintype. 1861

Young girl with a shawl. Tintype. 1868

Pioneer photographer Colwell Lane took advantage of the tintype label to indicate the scope of his professional ability. 1867

Carpenter and tools. Tintype. 1868

Theatre scene. Tintype. 1880

CLIMAX FERROTYPE CAMERAS.

		Without Lenses.	With Lenses.
No. 37½. Camera and shield for 4 on 1–4 plate with 4 1-9 lenses		$6 75	$16 00
" 38. " " 6 " 1-2 " 6 "		8 50	22 25
" 39. " " 9 " 5-7 " 9 "		12 00	32 50

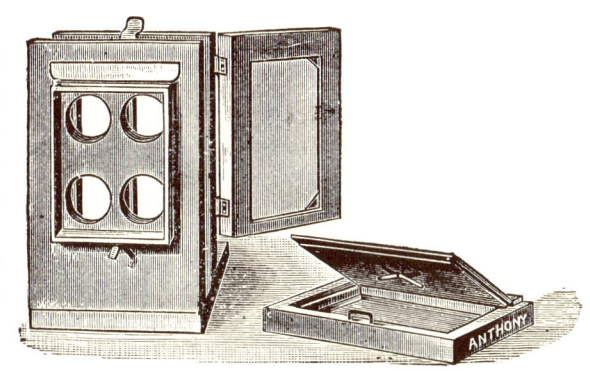

No. 41. This is an excellent and cheap camera for making four bon-tons on a 5 x 7 ferro. plate with four tubes, or one card or cabinet picture on a 5 x 7 plate with one lens.

Without lenses............ $12 00
Fitted with four 1–4 lenses. 27 50

CLIMAX OR NEW YORK GEM CAMERA.

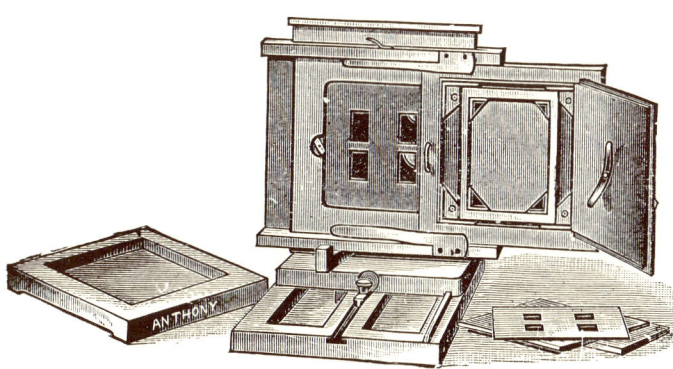

This camera has been in great demand for small ferro. work and photographs to half size.

	Without Lenses.	With 4 1-9 Lenses.
No. 42. For 4, 8 and 16 on 1–4 plate with 4 1-9 lenses, 2 on 1-2 plate, and 1-2 to 1-6 reversible with 1 portrait lens	$15 00	$24 00

Examples of tintype cameras from Buchanan, Bromley & Company's "Illustrated Catalogue of Photographic Materials," 1888 edition.

In this framed tintype and with hats in hand, these two young men pose proudly against a painted backdrop.   1869

Tintype label.   1865
E. S. Wormell,
Portland, Me.

When good friends get together   1870
...it's time to have a picture taken.

For these two brothers   1875
the occasion was new clothes.
Note the base of the headrests
in back of the men.

S. D. Moss (holding reins) and Coachman Charlie Jones photographed 1899
opposite Cranmer's Baths, Ocean Avenue, Long Branch. The tintype, like the
daguerreotype, produced a mirror image – hence the reverse lettering.

How many fair hearts beat 1885
faster for dapper young men
like these. The studio backdrop,
a painted scene, now replaces
the old white canvas cloth.

How daring it must have been 1885
to pose like this before a camera.
Again, the base of the headrest
is visible behind the chair.

MINIATURES,
Taken by
J. L. & H. A. Jordan,
Main Street, near State St.,
New London, Ct.

Wing's Ferrotype Card Mount. Patent Pending.

From
ADAMS'
Photograph and Ambrotype
ROOMS,
No. 271 Main Street,
(PIPER BLOCK,)
WORCESTER, MASS.

Made with Wing's Patent Multiplying Camera
ONLY
At GEO. W. GODFREY & CO.'S

SUNBEAM GALLERY
Over 81 Main Street, Rochester, N. Y.

J. N. BRENGEL
FERROTYPE
GALLERY,
391 Canal Street,
NEW YORK.
4 FOR 25 CENTS.

D. I. SALT'S
FERROTYPE ROOMS,
239 FULTON STREET,
Opposite Clark St.,   BROOKLYN.

4 for 25 Cents.

FROM
A. R. DAVIS'
New
PHOTOGRAPH ROOMS,
UNION BLOCK,
BIDDEFORD, ME.
Photographs from life and copied Small pictures of all kinds enlarged and finished in ink or colors, Carte de Visites, &c.

FROM J. D. POWERS'
PHOTOGRAPH SALOON,
SPRINGFIELD, VT.
Where small Daguerreotypes and other small Pictures are copied to large, making beautiful Frame Pictures, (portraits) colored in oil, water colors, or finished with India Ink. Other common work done to order.
ROOMS OVER THE SAVINGS BANK.

BARNETT'S
FERROTYPES,
Old No. 73 Fulton Ave.,
New No. 461 Fulton St.
Near Lawrence Street,
BROOKLYN.

COPYING WITH NEATNESS AND DISPATCH.
Pictures finished in a few minutes.
6 for 25 Cents.

FROM
TRASK & MARSTON'S,
No. 40, West Side,
North Eighth Street, Phila.

Made as well in Cloudy as in Clear weather.

Finished in Fifteen Minutes.

Prices, styles of photographs, types of cameras, truly much of the commercial history of photography is preserved on labels such as these.

Chapel, Kenyon College.   1866
Gambier, Ohio.
Carte-de-visite.
It would be interesting to know if this photograph
was taken by the inventor of the tintype,
Professor Hamilton L. Smith of Kenyon College.

    The vast majority of daguerreotypes, ambrotypes and, to a lesser degree, cartes-de-visite and tintypes taken through the years are studio portraits...formal or informal as the case may be. By the very cumbersome nature of the equipment and the photographic processes used in the early days of photography, the outdoor scene was an exception.

    On the other hand, just the opposite was true of stereographic photography. The three-dimensional capability of the stereo camera was particularly suited for outdoor (or vast interior) scenes rather than the limited confines of a small studio. Thus the stereographic camera has documented an era whose vast subjects were largely unrecorded by the other contemporary photographic processes.

The Stereograph

In 1838, a year before photography became a reality, Scottish physicist Sir Charles Wheatstone produced an experimental device which utilized the principle of stereoscopic vision. That principle, as Professor William C. Darrah plainly stated "..rests upon the fact that the two eyes see slightly different images when directed to a given object"*. Wheatstone's experimental device (which he named the "stereoscope") remained a scientific curiosity for almost a decade. The first "pictures" used in this stereoscope were line drawings of geometrical forms. The first attempt at photographic stereography is credited to French-born British daguerreotypist Antoine Francois Claudet in 1842. However, it wasn't until another Scottish physicist, Sir David Brewster, designed an improved stereoscope eight years later (which overcame the severe limitations of Wheatstone's first model) that stereography became more than just a scientific phenomenon.

What is a stereograph? A simple non-technical answer is: a pair of simultaneously exposed, almost identical photographs, mounted side by side which, when observed through the appropriate viewer (stereoscope), present a remarkable illusion of a single photograph in lifelike three dimensions.

The use of daguerreotypes in early stereographs was greatly restricted by one basic problem. Each daguerreotype was a unique photograph and mass duplication was not feasible. With the development of the collodion wet plate process, however, the stereograph became a commercial reality.

---

*See page 4: William Culp Darrah, STEREO VIEWS. A HISTORY
OF STEREOGRAPHS IN AMERICAN AND THEIR COLLECTION.
Times and News Publishing Co., Gettysburg, Pa., 1964.

At the Crystal Palace during the Great London Fair of 1851, England's Queen Victoria and Prince Albert were particularly intrigued and impressed when shown a number of stereographic views displayed for the first time. With such royal approval the stereograph was definitely "in" and was quickly and graciously accepted in every proper Victorian parlour.

An indication of the stereograph's popularity is best revealed by some surprising statistics found in Darrah's history of the stereograph in America. In a single year (1862), for example, one French and one English firm published a total of almost two million stereo views. It has been estimated that between 1858 and 1920 there were issued just in the United States almost four million different stereo views!

Daguerreotypes and positive glass views were among the first stereographs produced. Stereographic daguerreotypes views are unique and quite rare. Glass stereographic views are uncommon but obtainable. Since no Monmouth County, New Jersey, stereographic views were produced by these two early methods, it is the common card mounted views which are the primary concern of this book.

Although most stereo cards are generally uniform in appearance there are definitely many variations including square or round corners, flat or curved mounts, and differences in color and size of the card mount. These significant variations (photographic subjects notwithstanding) are determining factors in establishing the age, origin and rarity of individual stereo views.

Stereographic views were first introduced commercially in the United States by Philadelphia photographers William and Frederick Langenheim in 1854. Stereographic views for the next fifty years became part of the lifestyle much like the early Gramophone and radio and like television and the world of computers today.

A Langenheim label from a stereo view of Passaic Falls, Paterson, New Jersey published in 1858.

"...'Seems? — nay is.' This was the compliment given to stereographic pictures when they were first made, so realistic did they seem." Thus wrote author Henry Clay Price in his introduction to HOW TO MAKE PICTURES: EASY LESSONS FOR THE AMATEUR PHOTOGRAPHER, published in 1882 by the Scovill Manufacturing Company.

Henry Clay Price offered the following instructions for making stereographic views:

CHAPTER XIV.

STEREOSCOPIC PICTURES.

How to Make and Mount Them.—The camera used to make stereoscopic pictures should take a 5 x 8-inch plate in the holder, have an upright division through the center, and upon the front board a pair of matched view lenses screwed into the flanges. Such are the requisites for this special service. Make sure that the central partition, called a stereo. division, is fastened in place.

Some discernment is needed in selecting the subject for a stereoscopic view. If the camera points to a distant hillside, and there is no near object included in the range, the view will appear flat when seen through the stereoscope, and will not seem to stand out from the mount. There should be included in the image reflected on the ground glass a near as well as the more remote view. Some shrubbery, the stump of a tree, or any distant and still object will answer. Stereo. pictures made upon this principle have the most seeming actuality about them. If the two pictures seen upon the ground glass are exactly alike, it is a proof that the lenses in use are well matched. After focusing, put the plate holder up in place of the ground glass.

As it is essential to success that the exposure of the two lenses should be made at the same time, place the focusing cloth on top of the camera, falling over to cover the lenses, and keep the cloth tightly drawn over them. Pull out the dark slide and, as usual, lay it on top of the camera. Now, all is in readiness. Raise the focusing cloth quickly. Do this so that light will enter the apertures in the lenses simultaneously. After a proper length of exposure, drop the focusing cloth

64 HOW TO MAKE PICTURES.

over the lenses and replace the dark slide. Follow directions in Chapter IV. for the development of the plate, but use care not to get one side of it more intense than the other; in short, the negative should be treated the same as any other, until it is ready to be printed from. Take a piece of ground glass, a trifle larger than the stereo. negative, and upon it draw with a lead pencil the diagram shown in figure 30.

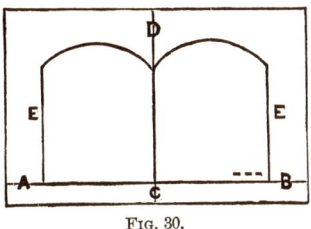
Fig. 30.

The distance between each of the lines E and the perpendicular $D\ C$ should be $3\frac{1}{8}$ inches, and from the base line to the crown of both arches, $3\frac{7}{8}$ inches.

These proportions make the very desirable size of stereo pictures, commonly called the "*artistic.*"

Lay the negative, film side up, upon the marked ground glass so that the right-hand half will come over the right-hand form penciled thereon, and *vice versa*. Take in the best portion of the subject. With care move the negative so that the line $A\ B$ will pass through similar objects in both halves; also adjust the negative to have the perpendicular $C\ D$ pass through defined lines or objects in the right half. With a sharp-pointed instrument scratch on the negative, using a straight-edged ruler, the line $A\ B$, also the line E. Shift the negative so that the perpendicular $C\ D$ will intersect points or objects corresponding to those in the other half. At the same time the scratched base line must coincide with, or be directly above, the line $A\ B$ on the ground glass. Now, scratch the left-hand line E, and the negative will be ready for printing.

All of the prints made will show a black base line, and the two outside ones, $E\ E$. Turn the prints face downward, and upon the back of the right-hand half mark with a pencil the letter L, and on the left-hand picture the letter R. Now, reverse the prints to have the face upward. It is to be hoped that you have available a glass form $3\frac{1}{8}$ inches wide by $3\frac{7}{8}$ inches high, with an arch top. Set down this form upon each print alternately, so that the lower edge will be on the line A

STEREOSCOPIC PICTURES.   65

B, and one side on one of the lines E. With a sharp knife or a *Robinson trimmer* cut closely around the form. The Robinson trimmer is suggested because it is so desirable that it has the commendation of photographers everywhere. Always cut the prints on a light of glass.

In mounting the prints on the card, put the one marked L on the left-hand side, and the one marked R on the right side, and have the two edges meet in the center of the card; also have an equal margin above and below the pictures. If you can avail yourself of a printing press or hand stamp with movable type, and choose to do so, you can print on fine tissue paper the name of the picture or locality of the view. In printing from the negative, this piece of tissue paper is laid on the face of the negative in one corner, so that the lettering will copy on to the print in the place shown by dotted lines on figure 30. Thin tissue or onion-skin paper will not prevent the printing of any part of the negative—the effect is to make the operation a slower one.

The instruction contained in this chapter will be pronounced quite elementary by men of experience. The reasons why have not been given, but enough is stated to enable the amateur to secure good results.

Indeed, the same is true of all that precedes, and I do not imagine that any one will think that he has mastered all there is in photography after fortifying by experience the teachings of this book.

The purpose is to enable the amateur to meet with success, and to furnish a stepping stone by which books more technical and profound will be made intelligible and interesting to the non-professional photographer. Very few, I think, will be satisfied with the rudiments of *this truly fascinating art.*

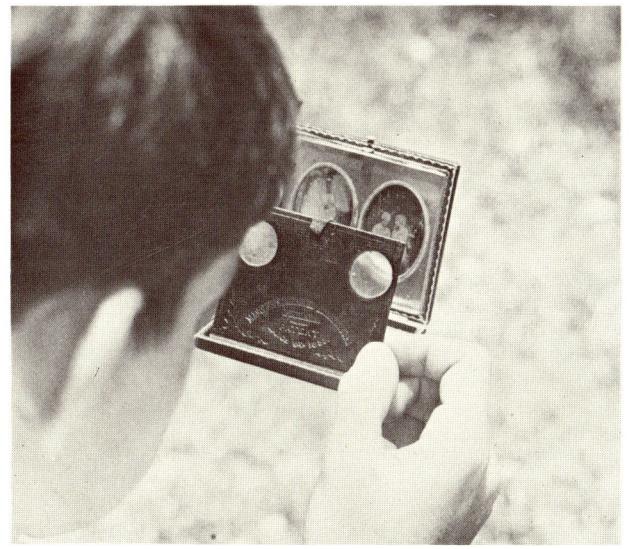

Philadelphian J. F. Mascher patented this combination stereoscope/daguerreotype case on March 8, 1853. The stereo effect is quite impressive as the pair of daguerreotypes of a marble statue blend into a single realistic three-dimensional object.

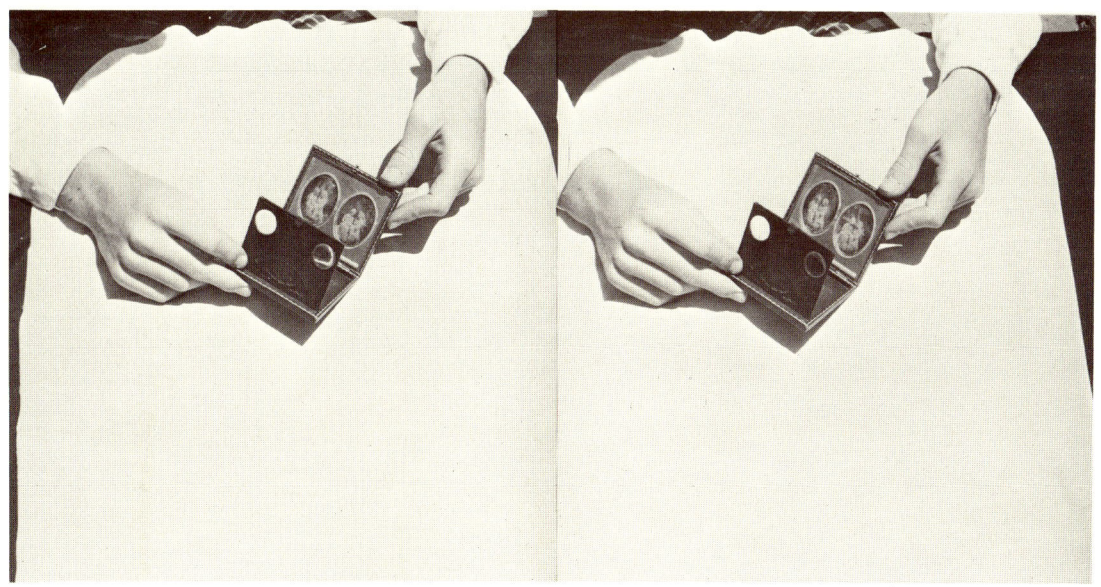

J. F. Mascher's combination stereoscope and daguerreotype case.
George H. Moss Jr., Rumson, N.J.

JUNE 12, 1970

A modern stereographic view of this rare stereographic item links one hundred and seventeen years of photographic history.

"*Suspension Bridge over Niagara River.*" *Glass stereo view.*
Babbitt & Tugby, Niagara Falls, N.Y.   1861

The exquisite beauty of a glass stereograph is enhanced by the clarity and extreme sharpness of the image.

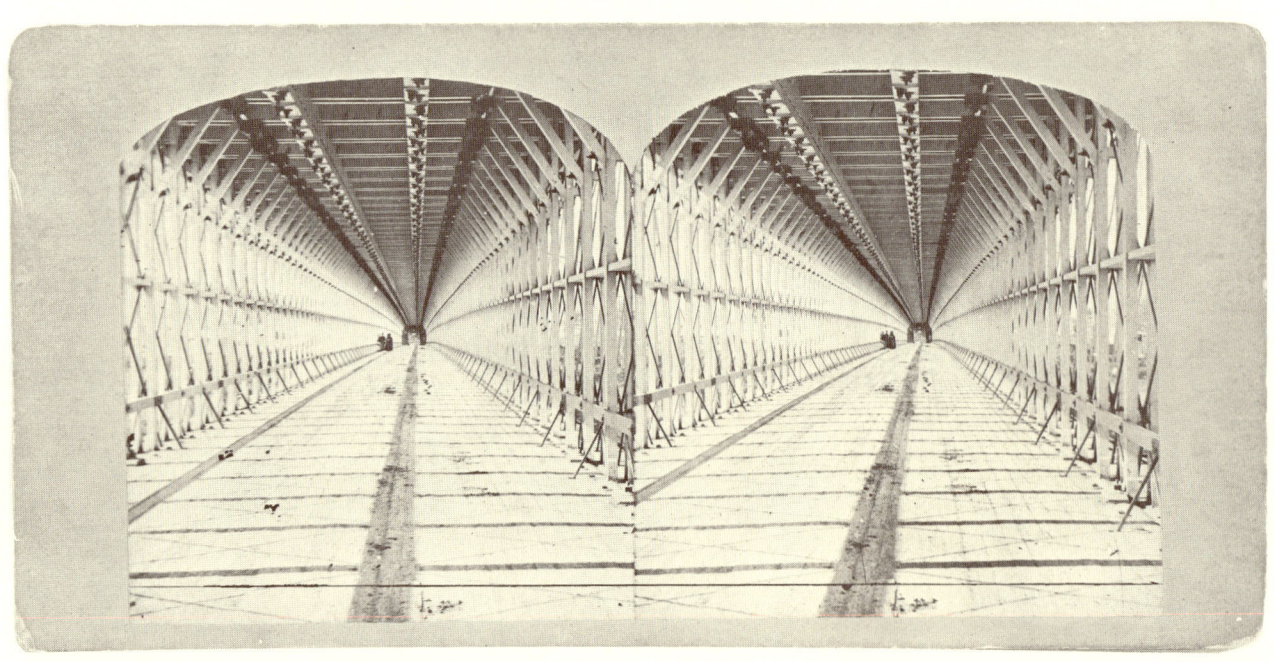

"*#70 NIAGARA. Suspension Bridge Interior.*"   VIEW 1862   CARD 1868

An unknown photographer, more than a century and a quarter ago, produced this dramatic interior view of the old Suspension Bridge at Niagara. The work of John A. Roebling of Trenton, New Jersey and first opened in 1855, the Bridge's top section was for the railroad while suspended underneath was the foot path and carriage road pictured here. The full capability of the stereo camera has been utilized to produce a spectacular three-dimensional image.

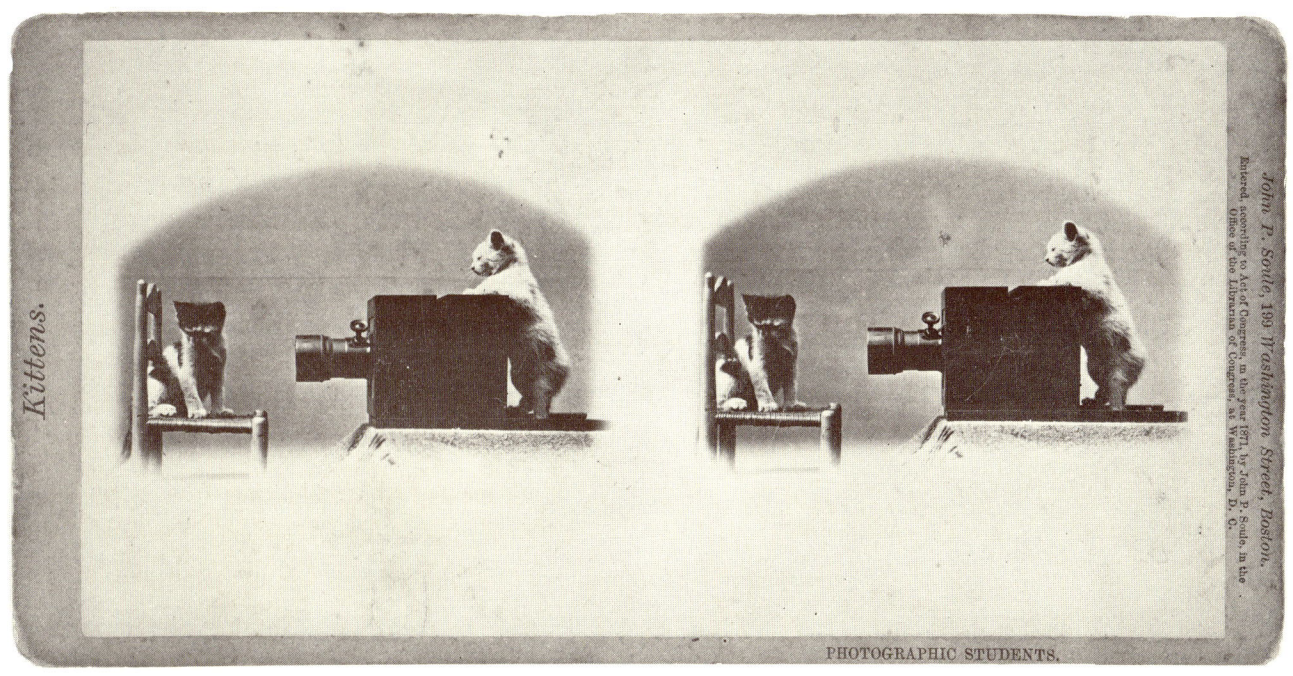

"Photographic Students." 1871
John P. Soule, Boston, Mass.

Kittens have always been an artist's delight. Incidentally, this three-dimensional view utilized two different cameras of the period: the standard camera with the kittens was photographed by the stereoscopic camera.

The pair of lenses perform the same function as a pair of eyes and create the illusion of depth perception.
HARPER'S NEW MONTHLY MAGAZINE. SEPTEMBER, 1869.

The standard view camera of a century ago. Some of the larger view cameras produced glass negatives greater than 20 x 24 inches.
HARPER'S NEW MONTHLY MAGAZINE. SEPTEMBER, 1869.

Two young girls (in 1970) view stereoscopic cards through a rare two way rotary stereoscope marked "A Becker, Pat. April, 1859. N.Y."

Fifty stereoscopic views, illuminated by sunlight from the open top, are mounted in pairs (back to back) on a revolving belt. This enables each youngster to look at one set of twenty-five stereo cards before before changing places.

A scarce and highly interesting volume, "Gems of American Scenery, Consisting of Stereoscopic views Among the White Mountains" was published in New York by Harroun & Bierstadt in 1878. It contains twenty-four stereographic illustrations printed by the Albertype process (patented by Bierstadt in 1876). The book is unique in that a quite adequate stereoscope is built right into a flap on the cover! An inspired example of book production from the stereographic era.

CROSS SECTION OF AMERICA

An infinitesimal segment of a broad cross section of America's history, the following twenty pages represent only a few of the thousands of significant stereo views taken during young America's great period of development and expansion: the Nation's Capitol Building under construction; a Florida backriver steamboat nudging it way up Orange Creek and an infant industry – the Oil Fields of Pennsylvania.

In the true sense of an overworked statement – only a stereograph can tell it like it was. Each view is an exciting three-dimensional vignette and important pictorial documentation of our Nation's coming of age. Places and events...some remembered, some long forgotten...leap from the printed page. With concentration and a little imagination one can almost hear the sounds of history...an urgent steamboat whistle at City Point, Virginia; shrill cries of excitement from merry skaters in wintery Central Park; a photographer's voice, "Thank You, Mr. President."

This was America.

"*New View of the Capitol, Washington, D.C. 1859*"
C.H. Wheeler & Co., Boston, Mass.

CARD 1863

An unusual view of the Nation's most recognized building while under construction – minus the familiar Dome.

U.S. Capitol, Washington, D.C. 1868
T.W. Smillie, Smithsonian Institution, Washington, D.C.

> For a number of decades prior to the introduction of the photo engraving process, photography played a major role in providing the leading illustrators of newspapers and weekly and monthly publications with pictorial subject matter. Pictured above, on an assignment near the Capitol, is a photographic van from "Frank Leslie's Illustrated Newspaper."

"Grant and Party at Clinton Ave." Martha's Vineyard, Mass. 1874
Possibly photographed by Joseph W. Warren.

> During the early part of his second term, much travelled President Ulysses S. Grant posed with friends on the porch of this flag-draped summer cottage at Martha's Vineyard.

STEREOGRAPH

No.

New View of the Capitol Washington D.C. 1859

— SOLD BY —

C. H. WHEELER & CO.,

5 & 7 Essex Street, Boston, Mass., U.S.A.

PROPRIETORS OF THE

BELLEVUE

STEREOSCOPE,

Patented Dec. 1, 1863.

This Beautiful Instrument has advantages not found in any other Stereoscope. It is nicely made in black walnut—with silver plated mountings.

Price $2. Sent by mail, post paid, for $2.40; or with six Stereoscopic Pictures for $3.75; or with twelve Pictures for $5.

A choice collection of pictures at $3 per dozen.

☞ Send for Circular.

C. H. WHEELER & CO.,

Nos. 5 & 7 Essex Street, Boston, Mass., U.S.A.

S. O. THAYER, Printer, Boston.

Congress Park, at Saratoga, N. Y., greatly improved and beautified since the season of 1875, is one of the most attractive of rural pleasure grounds. No park of equal size in the United States can be compared with it for beauty of natural scenery or elegance of architectural and artistic adornments. It is the property of the CONGRESS AND EMPIRE SPRING COMPANY, proprietors of the Congress and Columbian Springs, located within the Park, and of the Empire Spring and Saratoga Glass Works.

The **Columbian Spring** is a chalybeate mineral water, possessing active diuretic, tonic and alterative properties, especially valuable in liver complaints, dyspepsia, erysipelas, and all cutaneous diseases. As a tonic water, for frequent daily use, no spring is so popular as the Columbian.

The **Congress Spring**, discovered in 1792, is one of the most famous mineral springs in the world. It is an aperient or cathartic water, highly carbonated, of agreeable taste, improving and invigorating the spirits, appetite and general health in a remarkable manner. Its medicinal effects have been tested for nearly a century, and its use is prescribed by physicians with the utmost confidence, after long knowledge of its great efficacy, and *the entire comfort and safety with which it may be used*. To professional men and others whose occupations are sedentary, and to all sufferers from the various forms of bilious disorders, it is invaluable.

ANALYSIS OF CONGRESS SPRING WATER.

By Prof. C. F. CHANDLER, of Columbia College.

The sample of CONGRESS SPRING WATER, taken by me from the Spring, contains in one United States gallon of 231 cubic inches:

	Grains.		Grains.
Chloride of Sodium	400.444	Bromide of Sodium	8.559
Chloride of Potassium	8.049	Iodide of Sodium	0.138
Bicarbonate of Magnesia	121.757	Sulphate of Potassa	0.889
Bicarbonate of Lime	143.399	Phosphate of Soda	0.016
Bicarbonate of Lithia	4.761	Silica	0.840
Bicarbonate of Soda	10.775	Fluoride of Calcium	
Bicarbonate of Baryta	0.928	Biborate of Soda	each a trace.
Bicarbonate of Iron	0.340	Alumina	
Bicarbonate of Strontia	a trace.		
		Total	700.895

Carbonic Acid Gas, - - - 392.289 cubic inches.

GENTLEMEN:

A comparison of the above analysis with the analysis made by Dr. JOHN H. STEEL, in 1832, proves that the Congress Water still retains its original strength, and all the virtues which established its well-merited reputation.

Its superior excellence is due to the fact that it contains, *in the most desirable proportions*, those substances which produce its agreeable flavor and satisfactory medicinal effects—neither holding them in excess nor lacking any constituent to be desired in this class of waters.

As a Cathartic water, its almost entire freedom from iron should recommend it above all others, many of which contain so much of this ingredient as to seriously impair their usefulness.

Respectfully, your obedient servant,

C. F. CHANDLER, Ph. D.,

Prof. of Analytical and Applied Chemistry.

To the CONGRESS AND EMPIRE SPRING CO.,

SARATOGA SPRINGS, N.Y.

The label on back of Wheeler's view of the Capitol also provides both an illustration and price information about the scarce Bellevue stereoscope.

This label on the "Congress Springs" card is a magnificent promotional piece extolling the virtues of Saratoga's Natural Spring Water.

"Congress Springs." Saratoga, N.Y. 1876
Baker & Record, Saratoga Springs, N.Y.

A fashionable Saratoga Belle pauses and the elegance of an era is preserved.

Interior View, Restaurant, Flemington, N.J. 1875
Sunderlin, Flemington, N.J.

Less fashionable than Congress Springs, but no less important, is this sunlit view of a quiet lunch hour in an unhurried time. The wall menu offers patrons their choice of "Ice Tea 2¢ at meal, Milk 5¢, Pork and Beans 10¢, Preserved Quinces 3¢, Frankfurters and Sauer Kraut 12¢, Roast Lamb 13¢."

"Working the Dahlgren Gun – LOADING. Which will give an excellent idea of the mode in which this piece is managed."
Photographer unknown.

1861

Civil War Admiral John A. Dahlgren, commander of the Ordnance Department, introduced important improvements in naval armament and designed the gun that bears his name.

"909. The Great Union Meeting, Union Square, New York. April 20, 1861."
E. & H.T. Anthony, N.Y.C., N.Y.

A huge patriotic rally in support of the Union followed the Civil War's first engagement which resulted in Fort Sumter's surrender.

"2621. WAR VIEWS. General Hospital Wharf, Army of the Potomac, City Point, Va."   1864
E. & H.T. Anthony, N.Y.C., N.Y.

Sail and steam meet at the Army of the Potomac's supply depot on the James River.

President Lincoln's Funeral Procession in Philadelphia.   APRIL 22, 1865
Ridgeway Glover, photographer.

This rare view shows Lincoln's horse drawn hearse as it slowly moves along crowded Broad Street towards Independence Hall, Philadelphia. The black cloth canopy adorned with silver fringes and tassels is above Lincoln's coffin.

"The Great Central Fair, Philadelphia, 1864. ART GALLERY."
R. Newell, Philadelphia, Pa.

A rare indoor view of a Civil War fund raising event
and a fine example of the stereographic effect.

"Florida - Old Spanish House - Charlotte St. - St. Aug." 1886
George Barker, Niagara Falls, N.Y.

All eyes were upon New York photographer George Barker as he captured
the spirit of the moment in this quiet street scene in historic St. Augustine, Florida.

"565. Squaw and Pappoose – Luna Island – Niagara"
George Barker, Niagara Falls, N.Y.   1874

For decades this photographer was noted for his excellent stereographs of Niagara Falls and its surrounding area. In this view he has captured a peaceful moment between a Native American mother and her child.

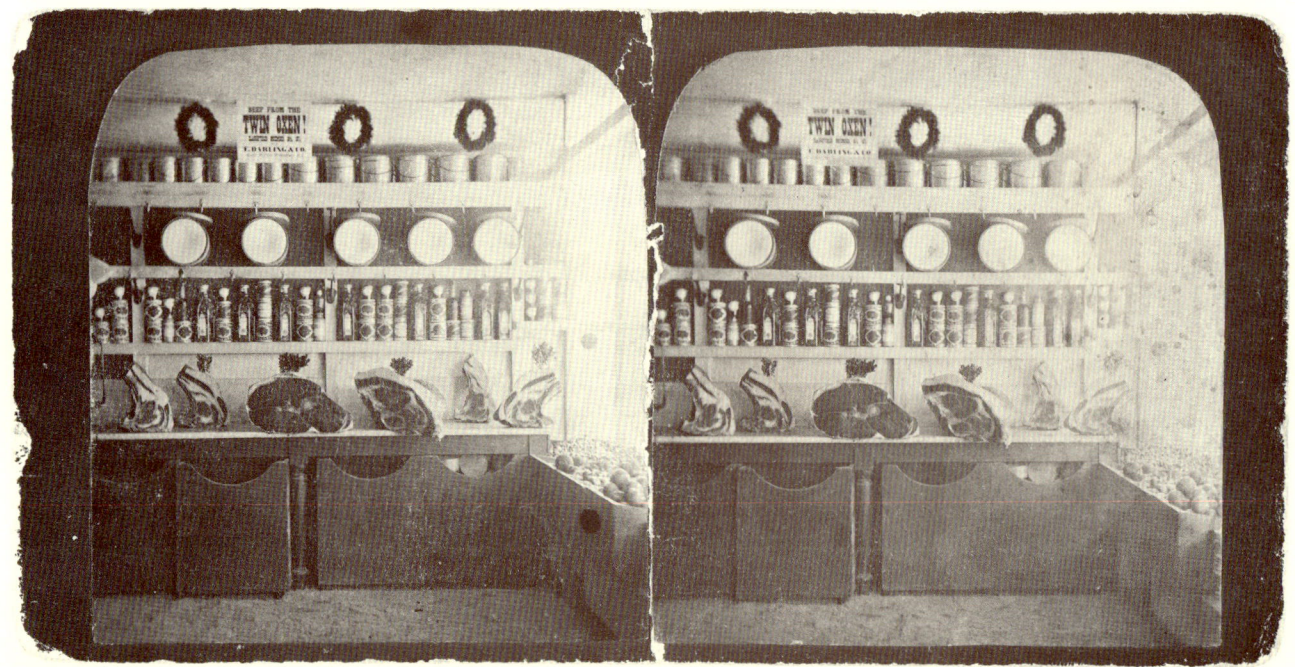

Interior of Eagle Market. Pawtucket, R.I.   DECEMBER, 1871

An obvious commercial view of this market shows exceptional prime cuts of "beef from the Twin Oxen!" as noted by the small sign in the photo…the story continues on the reverse side of the stereo card on the following page.

…this, the reverse side of the Eagle Market card, is truly remarkable. Here is an actual photograph of the prized Twin Cattle – and possibly of Lindley Horton of nearby Rehoboth, Massachusetts. The label tells the rest of the unique story.

"West side of East Temple Street." Salt Lake City, Utah.
C. R. Savage, Salt Lake City, Utah.

1875

Local city and town views are invaluable visual records of the past.

"60. Broadway, N.Y."
J. S. Johnston,
View & Marine Photo. N.Y.

1880

Telephone poles and tracks no longer exist on Broadway. Boxes of merchandise, however, still line the sidewalks of the commercial areas of the City.

"102. Principal Steamboat Landing." New Orleans, La. 1878
S.T. Blessing, New Orleans, La.

    Big two stack, stern wheel Mississippi River boats stand by while mule drawn wagon loads of cotton bales are brought to the levee.

55. "Suburban Group" 1875
F. A. Nowell, Photographer and Publisher, Charleston S.C.

    Seventy of Nowell's "Charleston and Vicinity" stereo cards are identified by number and title on the back of this truly suburban scene.

"Steamer Tuscawilla, at Orange Creek." 1873
America Illustrated, Tropical Series.

A unique photo of the "Tuscawilla." Looking more aground than afloat, this less than charming little steamer was a dependable workhorse on Florida's sluggish rivers.

"Lounging Saloon, Steamer Planet, Lake Superior" 1862
Photographer unknown.

Cheerful sunlight pouring through ceiling-high windows cannot overcome the seriousness of the moment - posing for a picture.

"First Well, Finkville, Penn." 1865
J. A. Mather, Titusville, Pa.

The birth of a new industry in the United States occurred with the discovery of oil in Pennsylvania.

"View No. 3 of R. R. Disaster at Milford, N.J. Oct. 4th 1877."
G. W. Freeland, Milford, N.J.

One of three stereographic views of this accident offered by photographer Freel and at 25 cents each. "Orders by mail promptly answered."

"Railroad Trestle Bridge, between 100th & 116th Streets, on Fourth Avenue, New York. View Looking North on Harlem."
Photographer unknown.

1868

The face of the city changes...as evidenced by this surprising view of Harlem.

"Skating Scene in Central Park, Winter 1866." N.Y.C., N.Y.
E. & H. T. Anthony, N.Y.C., N.Y.

This view is more like a Currier & Ives print than a photograph.

"Group of Shakers." 1875
James Irving, Troy, N.Y.

    A scarce and handsome portrait of members of "The Society of Believers of Christ's Second Appearing" probably photographed at Mt. Lebanon, New York.

Group Portrait. Niagara Falls, N.Y. 1874
Photographer unknown.

    Here, a family poses at Prospect Point as Niagara's rising mist forms an almost artificial backdrop. Framed samples of the photographer's art can be seen (at left) on a pole in the background.

"Wilcox Cottage, Sea View Avenue, Oak Bluffs"   1872
Possibly S. F. Adams, Oak Bluffs and New Bedford, Mass.

A small group of boys interupt their "tricycling" to pose for the camera in front of this fine row of Victorian cottages.

"157. The Fountain. Public Gardens."   1876
C. A. Beckford, Salem, Mass.

A quiet game of croquet does not disturb other visitors in this peaceful setting in the Public Gardens.

Storefront of C. M. Pettee.
Frank Z. Fritz, Lambertville, N.J.

A delightful formal portrait of both family and business. The storefront sign advertises "Pumps, Sinks, Lead, Iron and Terra Cotta Pipe." Mr. Pettee, with his dog at his feet, poses next to an artistic display of pipe joints.

"Tiffany and Co., 550 and 552 Broadway, New York."   1870
(G. W. Pach, N.Y.C.)

Founded in 1837, Tiffany & Co. was listed in an 1858 New York City Directory as "Importers and Manufacturers of Watches, Jewelry, Silverware and Fine Bronzes, etc." The Company was located at 550 Broadway from 1854 until November of 1870.

George Pine's Photographic Art Gallery.
27 & 29 East State Street, Trenton, N.J.
George Pine, Trenton, N.J.

1875

>In various locations in Trenton, including 25 West State Street, Pine Brothers produced hundreds of superb views of the area for many years. Later, George Pine became the sole proprietor. In the stereograph below, Pine's Studio interior displays examples of the work of this important New Jersey photographic firm.

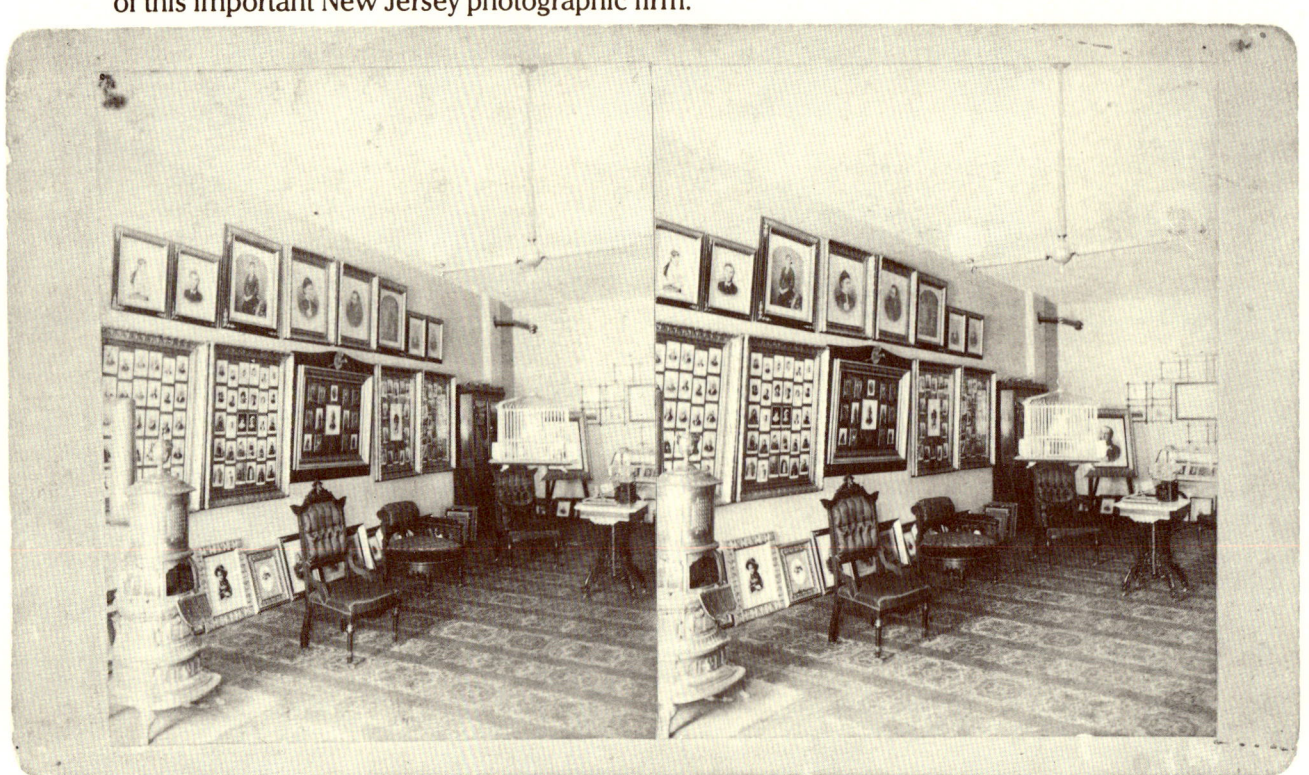

"Interior of Pine's Studio."
27 & 29 East State Street, Trenton, N.J.
George Pine, Trenton, N.J.

1875

"Floating Photograph Gallery" of J. P. Doremus. 1872
J. P. Doremus, Paterson, N.J.

New Jersey photographer J. P. Doremus took a series of interesting views along the Mississippi River after building this floating gallery to accomplish his mission. Note the skylighted studio amidship and the wall-displayed photographs behind the woman seated on the forward deck. The skylighted studio was necessary, afloat or ashore, for sunlight was the light source. The studio also housed many of the props needed to complete the artistic touch...including headrests to hold subjects motionless.

The next two pages illustrate typical stereo card labels. Since stereo card catalogues are almost non-existent, the labels are often the only available records of an individual photographer's stereo work.

The subscriber has built a Floating Photograph Gallery, at a cost, with its appurtenances, of over $4000, intending to take views of the Mississippi, and its tributaries, from the Falls of St. Anthony to the Gulf of Mexico.

The following comprise the Second Series.

30. View of St. Paul, Minn.
31. Levee at St. Paul, Minn.
32. Sights and Shadows of City Life, St. Paul, Minn.
33. The house among the Willows, St. Paul, Minn.
34. St. Paul Bridge across the Mississippi.
35. View of Hastings, Minn.
36. Railroad Bridge across the Mississippi at Hastings.
37. Steam Packet Minnesota at Hastings.
38. View of Point Douglas, Wis. Dudley's Island in the distance.
39. View of Prescott, Wis.
40. Pine Cooley, two miles below Prescott, Wis.
41. Levee at Taylor's Falls on St. Croix River.
42. Doremus' Gallery at Taylor's Falls Levee.
43. Dalles of the St. Croix.
44. Rustic Bridge, near Taylor's Falls Levee.
45. Devil's Chair in the Dalles of the St. Croix.
46. Devil's Chair and St. Croix Landing.
47. Steamer Nellie Kent at Taylor's Falls Landing.
48. Steamer Osceola at Taylor's Falls Landing.
49. Bridge between Taylor's Falls and St. Croix Falls.
50. View of the village of Taylor's Falls from St. Croix Falls.
51. St. Croix Falls.
52. Churchill Falls, near St. Croix Falls.
53. Turning Mill at St. Croix Falls.
54. Doremus' Gallery at Osceola, Wis.
55. Cascade Falls at Osceola.
56. Levee at Stillwater.

The subject on this card is indicated by a mark under the name and number.

J. P. Doremus, Photographer, Paterson, N. J.

The back of a stereo card served many purposes. Here, for example, it was a partial catalogue for J. P. Doremus of Paterson, N.J.

The title of this picture is underlined in the list below.

STEREOSCOPIC VIEWS
OF BORDENTOWN AND VICINITY,
Photographed and published by J. E. Smith, Bordentown, N. J.

1. Looking towards Canal from Com. Stewart's.
2. Looking towards Bordentown from Com. Stewart's.
3. Bennett's Store and Church Street.
4. South side of Main street, looking towards River.
5. North side of Main street, looking towards River.
6. Holmes, Shaw, Brown & Co.'s Machine Shop.
7. Canal Office and Surroundings.
8. Lower Depot.
9. Looking across the Del. from Black's Creek Bridge.
10. D. riv., canal and surroundings from Crescent Park.
11. Bonaparte's Park from Crosswicks Creek Bridge.
12. Interior Chair Car, built at Co.'s Shops, 1872.
13. Rev. J. H. Brakeley's College, once Tom Paine's residence, when the "Age of Reason" was written.
14. Bennett's Corner.
15. Lampson's Ship Yard, Molyneux's boats on stocks.
16. Capt. Smith Mershon's Residence from river front.
17. Canal Boat in Locks.
18. Interior View Christ Church, Thanksgiving services
19. Sand Dredging Machine on the Delaware.
20. C. L. Ice after the house was burned, Feb. 4, '75.
21. C. L. Ice after the house was burned, end view.
22. C. L. Ice after the house was burned, upper view.
23. C. & A. R. R. Shops, [now P. R. R.,] from river.
24. Thompson & Mott's Machine Shops, from river.
25. Bordentown in sections from ice on river, Sec. 1.
26. Bordentown in sections from ice on river, Sec. 2.
27. Bordentown in sections from ice on river, Sec. 3.
28. Bordentown in sections from ice on river, Sec. 4.
29. Ice breaking up at Bordentown, Scene 1.
30. Ice breaking up at Bordentown, Scene 2.
31. Ice breaking up at Bordentown, Scene 3.
32. Ice breaking up at Bordentown, Scene 4.
33. Ice breaking up at Bordentown, Scene 5.
34. Ice breaking up at Bordentown, Scene 6.
25. Main St. Snow Scene, Monday morning, Mar. 8, '75.

J. E. Smith of Bordentown, N.J., listed the titles of twenty-five of his stereographs. This invaluable resource also included the dates when some of these views were photographed.

PINE BROTHERS,
LANDSCAPE PHOTOGRAPHERS,
No. 25 West State Street, Trenton, N. J.

Dwellings, Store Houses, Manufactories, Stereoscopic Views, and Out-door Scenery of every description taken to Order.

Orders from City or Country will receive Prompt Attention.

CALL AND SEE SPECIMENS.

1875

Pine Brothers of Trenton, N.J., found the back of their stereo cards a dignified place for proclaiming their photographic capabilities.

GENT'S FURNISHING GOODS,
WHITE and COLORED DRESS SHIRTS for 50c., 75c., $1.00, $1.25 and $1.50.

2 Linen Collars for 25c.   Half Hose from 4c. to 50c. a Pair.

Men's, Ladies & Children's Underwear from 20c. to $1.50. Ladies & Children's Stockings, 4c. to $1.00.

SUSPENDERS FROM 10c. TO $1.50.   PAPER COLLARS 5c. A BOX.

Umbrellas for 40c., 50c., 65c., 75c., 85c., 95c., and $1.00 to $10.00

Revolvers from $1.25 to $15.00.   Double=barrelled Shot Guns, $5.00 to $100.00.

FINE ENGLISH PEN KNIVES and RAZORS for 50c.   POCKET BOOKS, 5c. to $3.00.

Knit Jackets from 85c. to $3.00.   Overalls from 35c. to $1.00.

AT A. W. LEE'S VARIETY STORE AND 50 CENT WINDOW,

48 GREENE ST., TRENTON, N. J.

U. S. Stereo. View Adv'g Co., 1217 Market St., Phila, Pa. ED. TRUST, Gen'l Mang'r.

Trenton Leading Business House.

1877

The U.S. Stereo View Advertising Company sold space on the backs of stereo cards. This display for a Trenton variety store is a typesetter's dream (or nightmare). There are fourteen different type styles on this single card.

79

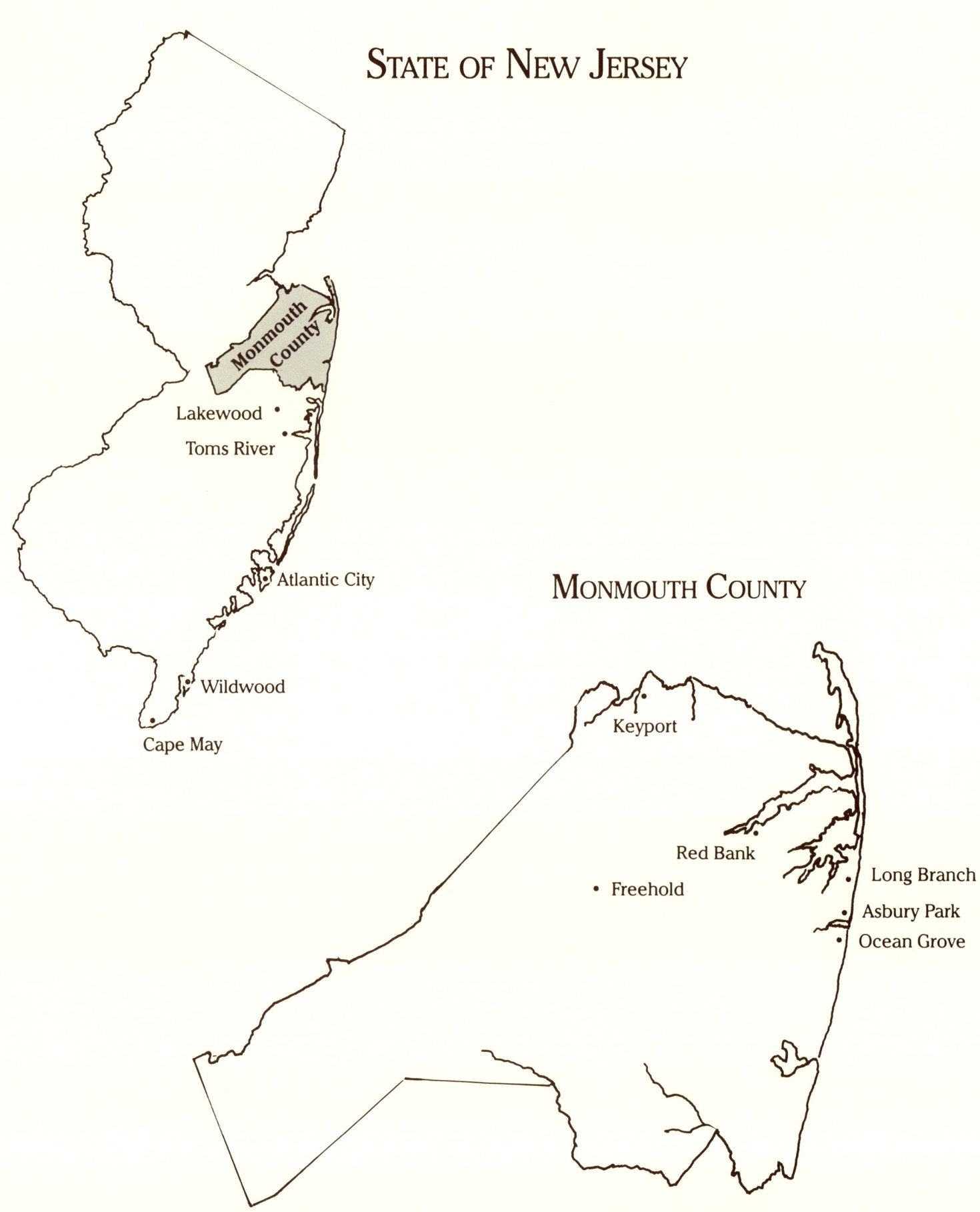

AT A LOCAL LEVEL...1859-1910

The Jersey Shore was America's playground and the face of America was recorded here, too. Therefore, equally important to our photographic heritage are the relatively scarce early stereographic views of the Jersey Shore.

Of the almost fifteen thousand American photographers in business between 1859 and 1889, about six thousand produced stereographs. Of the almost one hundred local Monmouth County photographers in business during that period, only eight are known to have produced stereographic views of the area. Between 1859 and 1910, it appears a total of little less than thirty photographers and or publishers, nationwide, produced stereo views of Monmouth County. At least another thirty stereographers photographed the rest of the Jersey Shore.

The eight local individuals who are known to have produced Monmouth County views include:

NAME	MONMOUTH COUNTY STUDIOS
DAVID N. CARVALHO	Red Bank
COLWELL LANE	Red Bank, Long Branch
WILLIAM H. HILL	Asbury Park, Long Branch
FERRIS C. LOCKWOOD	Freehold
GUSTAVUS W. PACH	Ocean Grove, Long Branch
SETH SHEAR	Asbury Park, Bradley Beach
SHEAR BROTHERS	Eatontown
WILLIAM H. STAUFFER	Asbury Park, Long Branch

Of these individuals, Long Branch photographer Colwell Lane should be acknowledged as possibly having the earliest photographic studio in the area. Civil War tax stamps (issued between September 1, 1864 and August 1, 1866) found affixed to many of Lane's early photographs, the popular carte-de-visite, indicate he was in business prior to August of 1866. In spite of that early date it was not until about 1871 that Lane, working with David N. Carvalho, first issued stereo views under the name of the New Jersey Stereographic View Company.

However, it is G. W. Pach, also from Long Branch, who must be credited as the first known Monmouth County photographer to publish stereographic views. His earliest stereo views were probably produced by 1868.

Two Asbury Park photographers: William H. Stauffer (who also had a Trenton, New Jersey studio) and William H. Hill (who had his major studio in Elizabeth, New Jersey, and one in Long Branch) were both popular in the early 1880's. Little is known of Asbury Park photographer Seth Shear (who also had a Florida studio) or of Shear Brothers (with an Eatontown address). With few exceptions, Freehold photographer Ferris C. Lockwood concentrated mostly on views of the western part of Monmouth County in the mid 1870's.

Of these local photographers, G. W. Pach produced the most stereographs of Monmouth County by far. David Carvalho and Colwell Lane's "The New Jersey Stereographic View Company" and William H. Stauffer would have to be considered the next two prolific producers of local views.

The rest of the other photographers and publishers of Monmouth County views had their business operations in other parts of New Jersey as well as New York, Pennsylvania, New Hampshire and Illinois. Most of these were the larger nationally known stereo companies whose vast stock of view cards covered a tremendous variety of pictorial subjects.

Of this group, the New York City firm of E. Anthony and Company produced the earliest known stereographic views of Monmouth County. In 1859, they issued three Long Branch beach scenes and a magnificent set of seventeen views called "Up and Down the Shrewsbury." Fifty-one years later The Keystone View Company produced some of the last commercial stereo views of Monmouth County when they photographed the 1910 Asbury Park Aviation Meet.

The Littleton View Company of New Hampshire purchased a number of G. W. Pach's views and issued them under their own name. Kilburn Brothers, another New Hampshire company, also published a few views of Long Branch while the Continent Stereoscopic View Company of New York published about a dozen Spring Lake and Monmouth Park stereographs. P. F. Weil reissued, purchased and even pirated views of other companies. Some of G. W. Pach's stereographs were published under Weil's name.

Pioneer Trenton cameraman Luther R. Cheeseman took a number of early views in the Freehold area as did Ferris C. Lockwood. Another half dozen minor publishers also issued various (often pirated) stereographs of Monmouth County and are included in this work.

How many stereographic views of Monmouth County were actually published between 1859 and 1910? An exact count is virtually impossible. However, for the moment, a little better than fifteen hundred different views seems to be a realistic and extremely conservative estimate.

The two sections that follow are [1]: the photographers and publishers of Monmouth County stereo views and a listing of almost seven hundred examples of their work produced between 1859 and 1910 and [2]: a first attempt to list photographers and publishers of this same period who documented the rest of the Jersey Shore all the way to Cape May.

E. Anthony – E. & H. T. Anthony

Pioneers in the new field of photography, the Anthonys became one of the most important publishers of American scenes. This New York firm issued some 10,000 different stereographic views between 1859 and 1881. Thus, it is not surprising to find the earliest known Monmouth County stereo views listed in their early catalogues.

Major publishers of all types of photographs including the efforts of other photographers (including many by Matthew Brady), E. and H. T. Anthony were also suppliers of photographic chemicals and equipment. An interesting footnote to the company's history is that as a result of various business mergers the Agfa ANSCO Corporation became a lineal descendant of the E. and H. T. ANthony Company and the SCOvill and Adams Company.

Edward Anthony had been in the photographic business in the 1840's, virtually from the start of the industry in the United States. His New York City firm moved from 308 to 501 Broadway in 1860. In 1871 the firm moved again, this time to 591 Broadway, where it remained for a decade. Knowledge of business addresses are often an aid in approximating the publication date of a photograph.

Most Anthony stereographs are particularly pleasing to view. Excellent choices of a wide variety of subjects and the artistic ability to capture the natural beauty of a scene has produced some exceptionally esthetic documentary results. While a great number of the Anthony views are of considerable historic importance nationally, many of their views at the local level are especially significant. The twenty Monmouth County views of 1859-60 are a case in point.

A carte-de-visite of celebrated American actress Maggie Mitchell. A Long Branch, N.J. resident for many years, her best remembered roles were in "Fanchon the Cricket" and "Jane Eyre." (From a Matthew Brady negative published by E. & H.T. Anthony between Sept. 1, 1864 and Aug. 1, 1866.)

ANTHONY'S INSTANTANEOUS VIEWS, STEREOSCOPIC, ARE NOW READY FOR SALE.

The following are some of the subjects:

The Regatta July 4th, 1859.	View of the Police on the Battery, July 4th, 1859.
Waiting for the Regatta.	Broadway alive
Crowd leaving after the Regatta	Propeller at Full Speed.
Steamship Quaker City coming up the Bay.	Niagara, Horse Shoe Fall.
Schooner under full Sail.	Niagara, the Rapids.
Ferry Boat running to Staten Island.	Niagara, Group of Children Viewing the Falls.
Steamer Sylvan Shore.	Niagara, Cave of the Winds.
Omnibuses Arriving and Departing, South Ferry.	Up Broadway on a Rainy Day. Down Broadway on a Rainy Day.

Together with many other interesting Scenes. New Pictures are constantly being added.

THESE VIEWS HAVE SURPRISED EVERYBODY WHO HAS SEEN THEM.

OBJECTS IN RAPID MOTION are depicted as sharply and distinctly as if they had been transfixed for the purpose

No visitor should leave New York without some of them to astonish friends at Home.

E. ANTHONY, 308 Broadway.

A full assortment of American and Foreign Views, always on hand and constantly replenished. 197

On September 10, 1859, Frank Leslie's Illustrated Newspaper displayed Edward Anthony's first advertisement for stereoscopic views.

Instantaneous stereoscopic views of rapidly moving objects were introduced by E. Anthony in this advertisement. The "ad" also reveals the vast subject matter published by Anthony in 1859/60.

STEREOSCOPIC THE WORLD IN MOTION.

ANTHONY'S INSTANTANEOUS STEREOSCOPIC VIEWS,

Showing Vivid Pictures of rapidly moving objects, Steamers, Ships, Railroad Cars, Vehicles, Regattas, Life in Broadway, Water Falls, Niagara, the Rapids, &c., &c. Taken by a process of our own invention, and now just ready for sale

Views in America, England, Ireland, Scotland, Wales, Paris, Brittany, Normandy, Spain, Switzerland, Italy, Russia, Turkey, Greece, the Holy Land, Egypt, India, Germany and Belgium; also, Views of Cherbourg, the Camp de Chalons, Versailles, Fontainebleau, the Seats of English Nobility, the Crystal Palace, Sydenham, and various other places of interest.

Fine Statuary, Fruit and Flower Pieces, Coral and Game, Illuminated Interiors and Exteriors Dioramics (very beautiful), Cattle Scenes, Marriage Scenes, Breakfast Scenes, Pic nics, Rustic Groups, Elliott's best Groups, Sylvester's best Groups, Historical Pictures, Sacred Subjects, Humorous Subjects, Illustrations of Beranger, Illustrations of La Fontaine, Shells.

Attention is particularly called to our fine Views on Glass of places of classic interest, some of which should be possessed by every person of refined and cultivated taste —the ruins of Egypt, Greece, Rome, Italy, Spain, the Rhine, &c., &c., &c.

STEREOSCOPES

Of every quality, from the cheapest to those exhibiting 25 and 100 views.

OUR AGENTS IN LONDON AND PARIS

Keep us constantly supplied with the latest and best Stereoscopic Pictures.

Circulars with further particulars sent to any address on application.

Orders will be attended to with great care. As good an assortment, and at as low prices may be depended upon by ordering through the mail as by attendance in person.

E. ANTHONY, 308 Broadway.

Importer and Manufacturer of

PHOTOGRAPHIC MATERIALS FOR AMATEURS AND THE TRADE.

☞ This is the only large house in the United States, whose attention is exclusively devoted to Photographic Materials and Stereoscopy. 193 205

STEREOSCOPIC VIEWS OF THE WAR!

Obtained at great expense and forming a complete PHOTOGRAPHIC HISTORY OF THE GREAT UNION CONTEST.

Bull Run,	Nashville,
Yorktown,	Strawberry Plains,
Gettysburg,	Deep Bottom,
Fair Oaks,	Belle Plain,
Savage Station,	Monitors,
Fredericksburg,	Chattanooga,
Fairfax,	Fort Morgan,
Dutch Gap,	Atlanta,
Pontoon Trains,	Richmond,
Hanover Junction,	Petersburg,
Lookout Mountain,	Charleston,
Chickahominy,	Mobile,
City Point,	&c., &c.

Everybody is interested in these memorable scenes.

Catalogue sent on receipt of stamp.

Just published by

E. & H. T. ANTHONY & CO.,
o   501 Broadway, N.Y.

E. & H. T. ANTHONY & CO., Manufacturers of Photographic Materials
WHOLESALE AND RETAIL
501 BROADWAY, N. Y.

In addition to our main business of PHOTOGRAPHIC MATERIALS, we are Headquarters for the following, viz:

STEREOSCOPES & STEREOSCOPIC VIEWS,

Of these we have an immense assortment, including War Scenes, American and Foreign Cities and Landscapes, Groups, Statuary etc., etc. Also, Revolving Stereoscopes, for public or private exhibition. Our Catalogue will be sent to any address on receipt of Stamp.

PHOTOGRAPHIC ALBUMS,

We were the first to introduce these into the United States, and we manufacture immense quantities in great variety, ranging in price from 50 cents to $50 each. Our ALBUMS have the reputation of being superior in beauty and durability to any others. They will be sent by mail, FREE, on receipt of price.

☞ FINE ALBUMS MADE TO ORDER. ☜

CARD PHOTOGRAPHS.

Our Catalogue now embraces over FIVE THOUSAND different subjects to which additions are continually being made) of Portraits of Eminent Americans, etc., viz: about
100 Major-Generals, 100 Lieut.-Colonels, 550 Statesmen,
200 Brig.-Generals, 250 Other Officers, 130 Divines,
275 Colonels, 75 Navy Officers, 125 Authors,
40 Artists, 125 Stage, 50 Prominent Women,
3,000 Copies of Works of Art

including reproductions of the most celebrated Engravings, Paintings, Statues, etc. Catalogues sent on receipt of stamp. An order for One Dozen PICTURES from our Catalogue will be filled on the receipt of $1.80, and sent by mail, FREE.

Photographers and others ordering goods C. O. D. will please remit twenty-five per cent. of the amount with their order.

☞ The prices and quality of our goods cannot fail to satisfy.

Soldiers' Pocket Albums for 18 Pictures, 75 cents.

24 Pictures, $1 00.

The wide-spread interest in the photographic coverage of the Civil War is best indicated by these E. & H.T. Anthony advertisements found in the April 29, 1865 issue of Harper's Weekly.

ANTHONY'S INSTANTANEOUS VIEWS
"Entered According to Congress 1859"

15. "Shore and Ocean at Long Branch, with Vessels in the Distance"
15. also issued without copyright line on card.
17. "Bathing Scene at Long Branch"

E. ANTHONY VIEWS
308 Broadway, N.Y.

25. "At Long Branch, Overtaken by the Surf"
25. also issued without Anthony label.

25. "At Long Branch, Overtaken by the Surf"
Probably photographed in mid-summer of 1859, this and #15 and #17 are the earliest known stereo views of Monmouth County.

On the beach and correctly attired in summer fashions of the period, visitors enjoy the refreshing late afternoon ocean breeze. The cool salt air was a luxury and, indeed, was the raison d'être for visiting the "Branch" during the hot summer months. The famous Long Branch Bluff is in the background.

E. ANTHONY
501 Broadway

"Series: UP AND DOWN THE SHREWSBURY
price $3 per doz."

606. "The Spot Where The Melons Come From"
607. "Papa's Little Darling"
608. "A Look Off From The Highlands"
609. "The Skipper's Home"
610. "From Under The Bank"
611. "A Bit of a Picture"
612. "Cattle on the Shore"
613. "The Weeping Willow"
614. "Hands in His Pocket"
615. "The Farmer's Open Gate"
616. "The Lamp That Gladdens the Homeward Bound"
617. "A Charming Spot for a Country Home"
618. "From the Captain's Piazza"
619. "A Quiet Bay"
620. "Bub Enjoys the Landscape"
621. "How It Looks at Low Water"
622. "Three Fair Daughters of Jersey"

NEW CATALOGUE
OF
STEREOSCOPES
AND
VIEWS,
MANUFACTURED AND PUBLISHED BY
E. & H. T. ANTHONY & CO.,
EMPORIUM OF
American and Foreign Stereoscopic Views,
CARD PHOTOGRAPHS OF CELEBRITIES,
And Photographic Materials,
501 BROADWAY, NEW-YORK.
THREE DOORS SOUTH OF THE ST. NICHOLAS HOTEL.

Always at lowest market prices.
Supplements to this Catalogue will be issued every month or two,
with additions and corrections.

This series, photographed by E. Anthony in 1859/60, was first issued on ivory colored cards. It was later published under the E. & H. T. Anthony, 591 Broadway label and issued on yellow cards.

608. "A Look Off from the Highlands."
A view of Sandy Hook from the Highlands of Navesink.

The semaphore tower pre-dates the present Twin Lights built in 1864.

621. *"How It Looks at Low Water"*

    On the far shore of the Navesink River, a small herd of cows are the focus of attention of these two young girls.

622. *"Three Fair Daughters of Jersey"*

    Three young ladies think summer thoughts as they gaze upon the Navesink branch of the Shrewsbury River at Red Bank.

> **"AMERICAN SCENERY – NEW JERSEY"**
> YELLOW CARD
> 616. (is "The Lamp That Gladdens
>   the Homeward Bound")
> 619. (is "A Quiet Bay")
> GREEN CARD
> – *"Shrewsbury River"* (is #606 "The
>   Spot Where the Melons Come From"
> – *"Shrewsbury River"* (is #616
>   "The Lamp That Gladdens the
>   Homeward Bound")

The "Up and Down the Shrewsbury" *series was reissued on both Yellow and Green "AMERICAN SCENERY - NEW JERSEY" cards without publisher's or photographer's name. The green cards were just titled* "Shrewsbury River."

"Shrewsbury River" (is Green Card #616 "The Lamp that Gladdens the Homeward Bound"). This is one of the earliest photographs of the historic Sandy Hook Light House, a beacon for navigators since 1764.

The series was again reissued on "AMERICAN SCENERY - AMERICAN SCENERY" cards. These yellow cards were also titled *"Shrewsbury River."*

> **"AMERICAN SCENERY - AMERICAN SCENERY"**
> YELLOW CARD
> *"Shrewsbury River"* (is actually # 617
>   "A Charming Spot for a Country Home")

Alfred S. Campbell

Elizabeth, New Jersey, photographer A. S. Campbell, although not a major publisher, issued many interesting New York and New Jersey views between 1892 and 1905. Of particular interest to Monmouth County are the five different views of the stranding of the ST. PAUL at Long Branch.

ALBERT S. CAMPBELL VIEWS

"215.   Yacht DEFENDER 1895" (off Sandy Hook, N.J. ?)
"271.   Yacht DEFENDER 1896" (off Sandy Hook, N.J. ?)

"Elizabeth, N.J., USA Copyrighted 1896"

"413.   AM. LINER ST. PAUL ON SHORE, LONG BRANCH, N.J., JAN. 1896"
"414.   AM. LINER ST. PAUL ON SHORE, LONG BRANCH, N.J., JAN. 1896."
"415.   AM. LINER ST. PAUL ON SHORE, LONG BRANCH, N.J., JAN. 1896."
"416.   AM. LINER ST. PAUL ON SHORE, LONG BRANCH, N.J., JAN. 1896."
"417.   AM. LINER ST. PAUL ON SHORE, LONG BRANCH, N.J., JAN. 1896."

"413.   AM. LINER ST. PAUL ON SHORE, LONG BRANCH, N.J., JAN. 1896"

Other stereographic views of this obviously popular newsworthy event were issued by at least two other publishers besides Campbell: Griffith & Griffith and a card labeled "STEREOGRAPHIC GEMS of American and Foreign Scenery."

Luther R. Cheeseman

Pioneer photographer Luther R. Cheeseman had his "Trenton Photograph and Art Gallery" at 27 East State Street in the early 1860's. He might have received his early professional training from a possible relative, Jona. F. Cheeseman, a Trenton daguerreotypist whose studio, in 1854, was located at 104 Front Street. Luther R. Cheeseman's series of Cemetery views of historic Tennent Church are nice examples of the quality so often found in the work of pioneer cameramen.

LUTHER R. CHEESEMAN VIEWS

Tennent Church Cemetery - distant view including obelisk
Tennent Church and Cemetery - distant view includes shed
Tennent Church and Cemetery - medium view
Tennent Church and Cemetery - close up
Tennent Church and gravestones - close up of Davis, Secor and other names
Tennent Church and gravestone close up of Martha E. daughter of Enoch and Margaret Cheeseman and wife of Forman Conover
Tennent Church Cemetery with man, two women and girl at grave site
Tennent Church Cemetery - long view of many gravestones and distant Church

Tennent Church Cemetery with man, two women and girl at gravestone.

Continent Stereoscopic Company

This New York City company, most active between 1875 and 1885, issued stereo views, standard photographs and even wood engravings of their own as well as many pirated stereo views. Located first at 60 Nassau Street, the firm moved to 194 Worth Street by the mid 1870's. An 1877 Continent Stereoscopic Company catalogue reveals a diversified list of titles. Particularly strong in Western views, the selections included Arizona, California, Colorado, Washington Territory and Alaska. It was the policy of the Company to purchase negatives from various sources for additional titles. Offered in this catalogue, for example, were thirty-one rare cabinet photographs of California taken in 1857.

Eight Monmouth County views were listed in the 1877 catalogue.

CONTINENT STEREOSCOPIC COMPANY VIEWS

1060.	"View at Spring Lake"
1063.	"Monument (sic) Park Hotel, N.J."
1090.	"Monmouth Park Hotel, N.J."
1108.	"Spring Lake Hotel"
1109.	"Group at Spring Lake Hotel"
1110.	"Band Stand at Monmouth Park"
1111.	"Monmouth Park Hotel"
212.	"Monmouth Park Hotel, N.J."

The cover of the Continent Stereoscopic Company's twenty-two page catalogue of 1877.

Griffith & Griffith

PHILADELPHIA, ST. LOUIS, AND LIVERPOOL, ENG.

One of a half dozen major publishers and distributors at the turn of the century, Griffith and Griffith mass-produced an impressive number of stereo views (including those of other photographers) between 1895 and 1917. One popular Monmouth County subject issued under their own label was the grounding of the steamer "St. Paul" at Long Branch. Although two different views, both cards have the same title and catalogue number.

> **GRIFFITH & GRIFFITH VIEWS**
> **"American and Foreign Views" series:**
> Same numbers - different views January, 1896
> "X345. S.S. St. Paul, Ashore at Long Branch"
> "X345. S.S. St. Paul, Ashore at Long Branch"

"X345. S.S. St. Paul, Ashore at Long Branch"   1896

This is a typical stereographic view of the event. Most photographers rarely showed the vessel's position in relation to the shore.

"Steamship St. Paul ashore at Long Branch, N.J. Feb 1896"
Photographer unknown.

This magnificent original (non-stereographic) 9 1/4 x 12 1/2 sepia toned albumen print is a photograph that clearly depicts the grounding of the Steamer "St. Paul" and its relationship to the beach, buildings and Ocean Avenue, Long Branch.

William H. Hill

William H. Hill maintained studios at 110 Broad Street, Elizabeth; Lake Avenue and Webb Street, Asbury Park and, for a short time, a small studio in Long Branch. Hill produced more than sixty Monmouth County stereographic views. Unfortunately, the cards are rarely numbered or titled. The majority of views were taken in Ocean Grove, Asbury Park, Spring Lake and Sea Girt.

While primarily documentary photographs taken in the late 1870's and early early 1880's, Hill's stereographs are of fine quality and extremely interesting. They capture much of the feeling of that era. Also, choice of camera angle and careful composition has resulted in above average dimensional effects.

WILLIAM H. HILL VIEWS
- "Sea-Side Home of the Philadelphia Home for Infants, Ocean Park, (near Ocean Grove), N.J."
- Asbury Park from Sheldon House
- Both Shores of Wesley Lake
- Calif. Big Tree" sign in structure
- Outdoor Auditorium, Ocean Grove
- Lake Scene, Ocean Grove
- Japanese Cottage, Asbury Park - 1878
- Asbury Park Pavillion
- Beach and Boardwalk, Asbury Park
- St. John's Island, Sunset Lake Asbury Park
- Hotel Bristol, Asbury Park
- Monmouth House Porch, Spring Lake
- Monmouth House, Spring Lake
- Front Stoop of Beach House, Sea Girt

[plus another thirty variant views of the above subjects]

An example of a William H. Hill Label taken from the back of the "Japanese Cottage."

1878

This bird's eye view from the Sheldon House captures some of Ocean Grove's tents and, in the distance, a number of Asbury Park's hotels.

"Japanese Cottage"   1878

A typical Hill stereograph of the period taken in Asbury Park.

95

Keystone View Company
Copyrighted Underwood & Underwood, Inc.
MEADVILLE, PA., NEW YORK, N.Y., CHICAGO, ILL., LONDON, ENG.

The Keystone View Company was, for more than seventy years, a major producer of thousands of stereo views. Absorbing many of their competitors, they became a giant in their field. While they issued a considerable number of New Jersey stereographs, the relatively few cards of Monmouth County are quite important.

KEYSTONE VIEW COMPANY VIEWS
- *"Aviation Meet. United Airship Company's dirigibile balloon. Asbury Park, N.J. 1906"*
- 11078. *"Baldwin Dirigible in Flight, Asbury Park, N.J."*
- 11776. *"Dirigible air balloon, flying over crowd at Aviation Meet, Asbury Park" 1910*

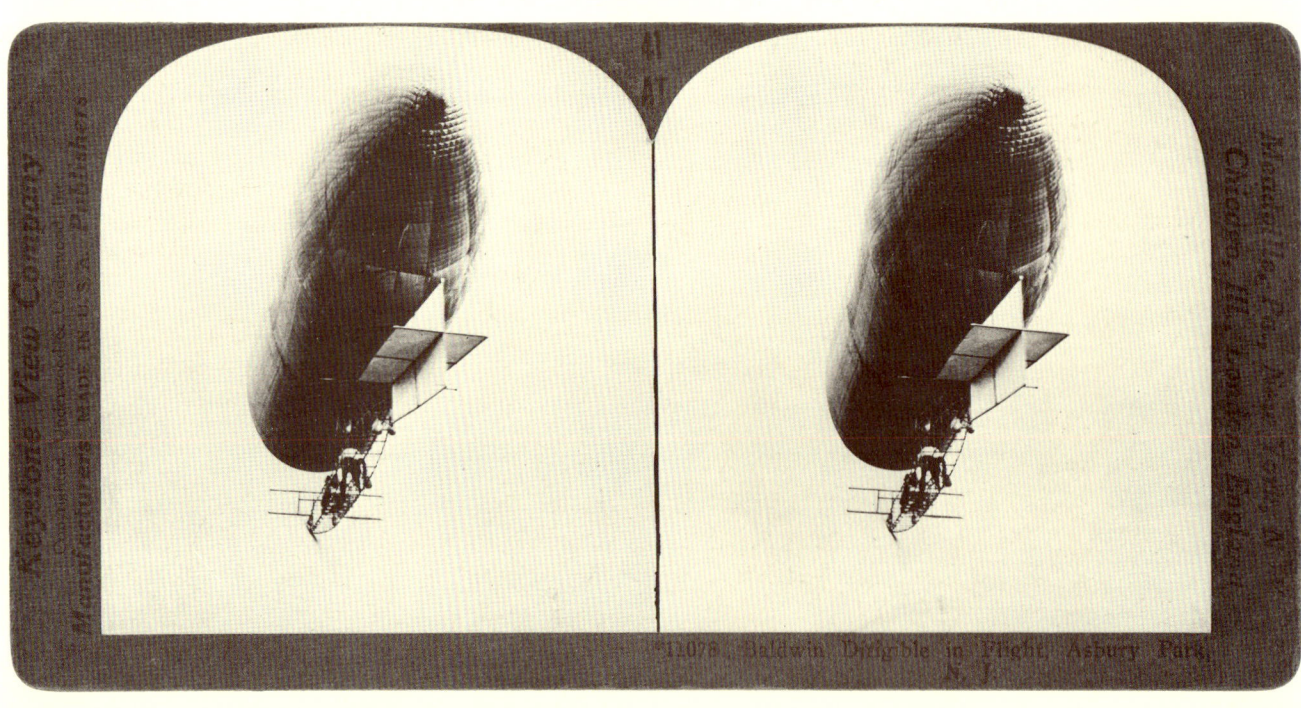

11078. *"Baldwin Dirigible in Flight, Asbury Park, N.J."*

Aviation Meets drew large crowds. Besides the early dirigibles, the Wright Brothers' plane was a special attraction flying low over the spectators at the Aviation Field.

Kilburn Brothers

Two New Hampshire brothers, Benjamin and Edward Kilburn, formed their own stereo view publishing company in 1865 in Littleton, New Hamphshire. Edward retired from the firm after a dozen years. Benjamin was the photographer for more than a decade. He actively continued the operation of the this popular firm until about 1904. The company produced thousands of stereo views until around 1908. All the original negatives were eventually purchased by The Keystone View Company.

Only three Monmouth County Kilburn views have been noted at this time. Considering the thousands of views issued b y the company, it is possible to assume there could be another six or seven local views. The missing titles in the number sequence would support that assumption.

Taken in the early 1880's, the two less than dramatic Kilburn stereographic views depicted on the following page are of particular interest because of their subject matter and the passing of time.

KILBURN VIEWS

"3132. The Garfield Cottage, Long Branch"
"3134. Bathing Beach, Long Branch"
"3137. The Little Bathers, Long Branch"

"3132. The Garfield Cottage, Long Branch" 1882

Mortally wounded in an earlier Washington, D.C. assassination attempt, President James A. Garfield was brought to Elberon, N.J., in a futile effort to restore his health. Garfield died on September 21, 1881 in this house which was also referred to as the Franklyn Cottage.

"3137. The Little Bathers, Long Branch," 1882

While a picturesque scene of three young girls wading hapily at the water's edge, through the passage of time, there is more significance in the background – the sidewheel steamer docking at the Iron Pier.

Littleton View Company

In business by the mid-1870s, this extremely popular New Hampshire stereo view company often published new titles by acquiring views taken by other photographers. This was not an uncommon practice. Earlier it has been pointed out that E. & H. T. Anthony, for example, published many of Matthew Brady's photographs. The Continent Stereoscopic Company also openly advertised for new titles in their own stereo catalogue.

Of particular interest, though, is the fact that apparently all of Littleton's Monmouth County views were stereographs originally produced from the Long Branch studio of G. W. Pach. The original Pach views, taken between 1870 and 1879 were reissued by Littleton a decade later. Where possible, Pach's original stereo number has been identified.

LITTLETON VIEW COMPANY VIEWS

1265. "Hoey's Grounds, Long Branch, N.J."
1266. "Gen. Grant's Cottage, Long Branch, N.J."
   (PACH # 88)
1270. "Sylvan Grotto, Long Branch, N.J."
1271. "Floral Gallery, Long Branch, N.J."
1272. "The Race at Monmouth Park, Long Branch, N.J."
   (PACH #71)
1274. "Young America, Long Branch, N.J."
1275. "Hoey's Grounds, Long Branch, N.J."
1276. "Hoey's Grounds, Long Branch, N.J."
1277. "Ocean Pier, Long Branch, N.J."
1278. "Hoey's Park, Long Branch, N.J."
1279. "Edwin Booth's Cottage, Long Branch, N.J."
   (PACH #48)
1334. "Ocean Pier, Long Branch, N.J."
1373. "Bathing Scene, Long Branch, N.J."
   (PACH #22)

"1272. The Race at Monmouth Park. Long Branch, N.J."

This is a reissue of Pach stereo # 71 originally photographed in 1870. In 1872, New York's Daily Graphic published a full page woodcut of Monmouth Park based on this stereo view. In 1883, a souvenir booklet of lithographic views of Long Branch used a number of Pach's stereo views (including this one of Monmouth Park) as the basis for its illustrations.

"1279. Edwin Booth's Cottage. Long Branch, N.J."

The home of one of the leading Shakespearean actors of the nineteenth century, this card is a reissue of Pach stereo # 48 taken in 1870.

"1274. Young America, Long Branch, N. J."   1884

The whole world was a goat cart for this youngster who smilingly posed for G.W. Pach while admiring friends stood shyly by.

"1334. Ocean Pier, Long Branch, N.J."   1882

The "Plymouth Rock" (pictured above) carried passengers between New York City and the Long Branch Pier. This Pach view was photographed in 1879.

Ferris C. Lockwood

F. C. Lockwood, the son of Reverend Samuel Lockwood, had a studio on Throckmorton Street, Freehold, New Jersey. He was perhaps a little more than a typical local photographer of the 1870's. Examples of his standard portrait work indicate he undoubtedly enjoyed a good reputation as a local cameraman. His advertisements stated he was an "ARTISTIC PHOTOGRAPHER. Out-door Photographs of all kinds made to order. Local Stereoscopic Pictures for sale."

His efforts, concentrated in and around Freehold, Monmouth County's County Seat, reveal him to be an astute business man, too. In 1872 he published a small eight page booklet entitled "For Parlor or Pocket, The Photograph Album, All About Photography." This delightful publication contained a capsule history of photography plus tips on what to do and wear when being photographed.

The Freehold area, while richly historic, was quite rural and certainly offered less stereographic opportunities than did the shore area at this time. Lockwood, to his credit, ventured out of his area to take stereographic views. He documented some newsworthy events including a set of views of the 1877 Keyport fire. Knowlegeable in his chosen profession, he contributed to a popular photographic journal of the day, "The Philadelphia Photographer."

FERRIS C. LOCKWOOD VIEWS

409.	"Keyport Fire. Sept 21st 1877 –West from Pavilion Roof"
413.	"Keyport Fire. Sept 21st 1877 – Atlantic Hotel Stables"
414.	"Keyport Fire. Sept 21st 1877"
415.	"Keyport Fire. Sept 21st 1877"
–	"Battle of Monmouth Relics"
–	"William R. Wilson, –Headstone, Tennent Church"
–	"Tennent Church & Cemetery"
–	"Tennent Church Interior"
–	"Tennent Church Interior"

An example of F. C. Lockwood's stereographic label.

F. C. LOCKWOOD,
Artistic Photographer,
THROCKMORTON STREET,
FREEHOLD, N. J.

No 409

"413. West from Pavilion Roof Keyport Fire Sept 21st '77"

This spectacular view of fire damage in Keyport in 1877 is one of perhaps a dozen stereographs of the disaster taken by F.C. Lockwood.

"Battle of Monmouth Relics." 1878

The bayonet, cannon balls and other relics of the June 28, 1778 Battle of Monmouth were probably photographed by Lockwood as a timely souvenir during the 100th anniversary of that historic moment in history.

Lovejoy & Foster

Most active in the 1870's, this Chicago firm was a major distributor for various mid-western photographers. One always popular New Jersey subject was President Grant's home at Long Branch. Lovejoy and Foster issued their own view of that well-known cottage by the sea.

LOVEJOY & FOSTER VIEWS
– "Gen. Grant's Cottage. Long Branch"

"Gen. Grant's Cottage. Long Branch"

One of the earlier views of President Grant's cottage with the President and possibly his son on the porch. A camera and tripod can be seen in the left stereographic photo (at the extreme right).

S. R. Morse

Atlantic City photographer, S. R. Morse published a number of fine views of New England, New York and Philadelphia in the 1870's and 1880's. It is possible these were reissues of other photographers' work as his Monmouth County views appear to have been first published by the New Jersey Stereographic View Company.

S. R. MORSE VIEWS

70. "Neptune Boat Club House, Highlands, N.J."
    (NJSVCo #70)
- "View of Lighthouse, Red Bank, N.J."
    (Sandy Hook Lighthouse)
- "View of Twin Lights." (similar to NJSVCo #53)
- "View of Pipe Foundry near Red Bank, N.J."
- "Cottage of George M. Robeson
    - Surf Road" Long Branch
- "US Life Saving and Signal Station" (NJSVCo #?)

"View of Pipe Foundry near Red Bank, N.J." 1875

Hardly an exciting photograph, nevertheless, when observed through a stereoscope it becomes a dramatic example of three-dimensional photography.

New Jersey Stereoscopic View Company

The "manufactory and office" of this company was located at the corner of Broad and Mechanic Streets in Red Bank, New Jersey. The company also had a photographic gallery at "5 Atlantic Block, Long Branch." This last address was the studio of Colwell Lane who began his Long Branch enterprise sometime prior to 1866.

An extremely prolific producer of cartes-de-visite, ambrotypes and quality ferrotypes, Lane became associated with another photographer, David N. Carvalho. They had formed the New Jersey Stereoscopic View Company around 1872. Carvalho was most likely related to Solomon N. Carvalho, the artist and daguerreotypist who, in 1853, accompanied Colonel John C. Fremont on his historic expedition to the Rocky Mountains. Solomon, in 1869-70, operated a "Portrait, Porcelin, Miniature and Photographic Gallery" at 765 Broadway, New York City. It is possible that the younger Carvalho learned his trade at this studio.

With Colwell Lane as President and David N. Carvalho as Manager, the New Jersey Stereoscopic View Company proceeded to publish over one hundred interesting and diversified numbered and un-numbered stereo views of Monmouth County (including a few Cabinet size cards). At least the same amount of views of Philadelphia and environs were published. Surprisingly, views of the Maracaibo area of Venezuela are found amongst numbered Monmouth County views. The Philadelphia stereo cards are imprinted: "From Negatives of the NEW JERSEY STEREOSCOPIC VIEW CO., 732 Chestnut Hill, Philadelphia and Long Branch, N.J. D. N. Carvalho, Manager. Published by JOHN F. JOY, No. 504 Callowhill St. Philadelphia." It appears that some of Lane's Monmouth County views were also published (pirated?) by other companies.

Colwell Lane was the first to leave the Red Bank company which evidently dissolved by 1876. Lane was in business in New York City from 1888 to 1890 at 145 Eighth Avenue. David Carvalho also moved to New York City where, from 1876 to 1887, he relocated his studio six times. In March of 1876 Carvalho applied for exhibition space in the Photographic Hall at the Centennial Exposition held in Philadelphia...as did G. W. Pach of Long Branch. While Pach was to later win an award, there is no further indication that Carvalho actually exhibited.

> LONG BRANCH.
>
> # C. LANE,
> ## PHOTOGRAPHER,
> ### MAIN STREET.
>
> Photographs, Cartes de Visite, Ambrotypes, Ferrotypes, &c., &c., taken in all weather, and satisfaction guaranteed.
>
> Work completed, finished up, framed and delivered promptly.
>
> A fine selection of Frames always on hand.

Colwell Lane's advertisement as it appeared in J. H. Schenck's "A Complete Guide of Long Branch, N.J." published in 1868.

> **Lane,**
>
> **Portrait and Landscape Photographer,**
>
> GALLERIES: { 5 ATLANTIC BLOCK, LONG BRANCH, N. J.
> { Cor. BROAD & MECHANICS ST., RED BANK, N. J

An example of Lanes' imprint on the reverse side of a carte-de-visite. Over twenty-three different types of Lane's imprints have been noted to date indicating a substantial production of this type of photograph over a long period of time.

NEW JERSEY STEREOSCOPIC VIEW COMPANY VIEWS

15 "Full Moon On Calm Surf"
18 "Cooper's Bridge, Red Bank, N.J."
50 "The Surf, Long Branch, N.J."
        (Seven women on beach)
50a Same photo-session as above
53 "Drawbridge Near the Highlands"
        (Twin Lights in view)
    Also issued on yellow cabinet size
        AMERICAN SCENERY card

54 "Drawbridge Near the Highlands"
        (close-up of bridge)
59 "The "Highland" Light-House" (front view)
60 "The "Highland" Light-House" (rear view)
64 "Island Beach from the (Highland)
        Light-House"
69 "Rustic Church Near Highlands"
        (Stone Church, Locust)
70 "Neptune Boat Club House, Highlands"
        Also Morse # 70
82 "Ocean Hotel, Long Branch"
        Ocean Hotel views 1872
82a Ocean Hotel Porch, LB
82b Ocean Hotel, Interior View
        – Bowling Saloon, LB
82c Ocean Hotel, Children's Pleasure
        Railroad, LB
88 "Atlantic Block, Long Branch"
89 "View Near Cooper's Bridge" Red Bank
124 President Grant and G. W. Child's
        Cottages, LB
125? President Grant's Cottage,
        Long Branch. Close-up
126? President Grant's Cottage
        (similar to 125?)
134 "Moonrise on Water"
136 Large Home. (Long Branch?)
137 Monmouth Park Grand Stand boarded up.
138 Dirt road and hill. Middletown, N.J.?
149 VENEZUELA "Street Scene in Maracaibo"
149a VENEZUELA "Maracaibo Indians"
149b VENEZUELA "Maracaibo Indians"

150 Two men lounging against Bluff. LB
150a Same two men walking near
        water's edge. LB
155 Dirt road, hilly, wooden fence, one man
184 Sandy Hook Light House. Man
        seated in path
–   Sandy Hook Light House and
        Keeper's Home
–   USLS Station. Galilee, Monmouth
        Beach, N.J. 1874
–   Ice Skating, Red Bank N.J. – A small group
        at river's edge. Red Bank, N.J.
– a Beach & Bluff. "West & Jeffrey, Bathers"
        sign LB
– b Same view as above. NJSVCO card:
        "1226 Chestnut Street, Philadelphia
        and Long Branch, N.J."
– c Same view on AMERICAN SCENERY card

–   Beach Scene. Many people. LB
–   West End Hotel OALB
–   5th Regiment, National Guard ? LB
–   Hoey's Park. LB
– a Close-up of Hoey's Mansion with
        five little girls. Same photo-session as
        next three views. LB
– b Hoey's grounds. Croquet game. Twenty-five
        children including same girls
        as above. LB
– c Seated picnic. Same group. Hoey's
        Grounds, LB
– d Same scene - distant view Hoey's Grounds, LB
–   Horse "Flora and colt"
–   Race horse and groom
–   "Uncle Mow and Windsor" Driver, sulky
        and trotter
–   "Mow G. and Black Watchman" Driver, sulky
        and trotter
–   Boy in chariot pulled by burro
Cabinet size
–   Presbyterian Church - Winter scene.
        Broad & Wallace Streets, Red Bank, N.J.

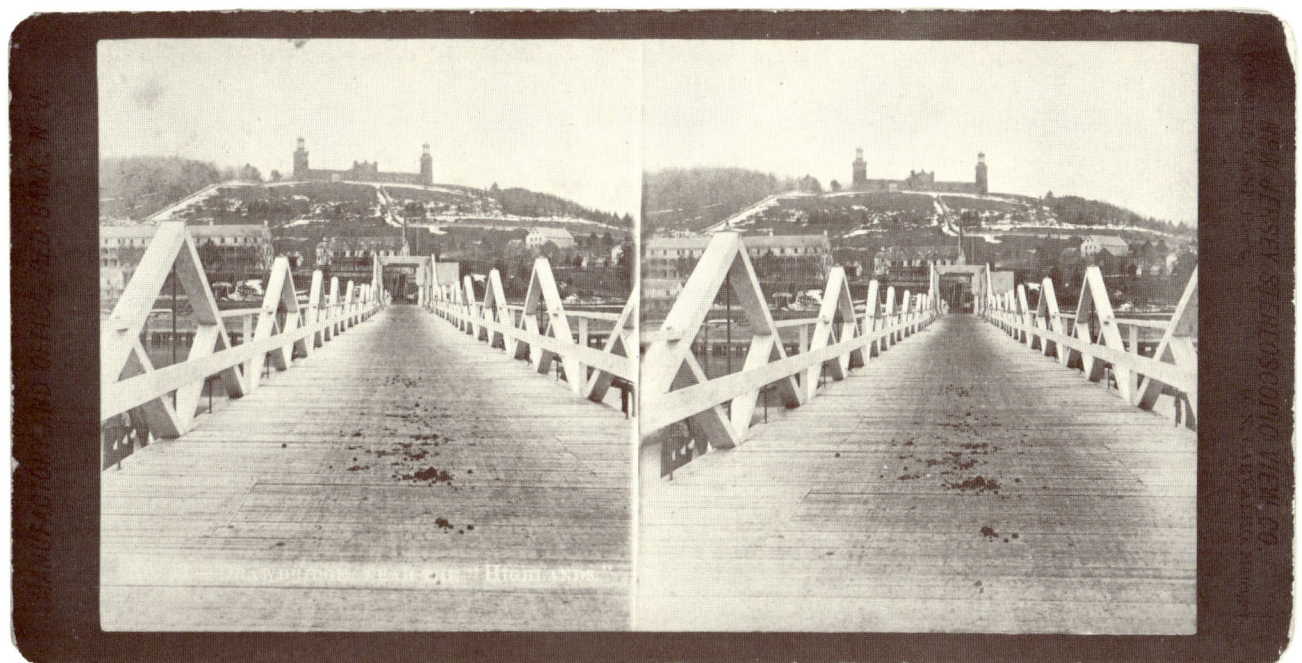

"No. 53. Drawbridge near the Highlands"   1872

Light snow patches and lack of foliage indicate this view of the Twin Lights was taken in late winter. The long structure at the left, Jenkinson's Hotel, offered summer visitors "River and Ocean Surf Bathing, Rowing, Sailing, Fishing, Crabbing" and proclaimed itself "surrounded by splendid shade trees."

"No. (71). Drawbridge near the Highlands"

This yellow, cabinet sized AMERICAN SCENERY card appears to be a special series by the NJSVCO. The original number (53) has been deleted and #71 scratched in its place. The backs of the AMERICAN SCENERY card lists almost fifty NJSVCO views of Baltimore, Philadelphia and Long Branch. See page 170.

"No. 89. View Near Cooper's Bridge," Red Bank, N.J.   1872

Foamy waves, the result of a strong wind, rush in along the banks of the Shrewsbury River. In the distance is Cooper's Bridge.

– "Group at River's Edge," Red Bank, N.J.   1872

Cool air and patches of snow on the landscape did not hinder this group from walking to the water's edge of the Shrewsbury River.

"No. 127 Monmouth Park Grandstand"

Probably photographed in the late Spring of 1873, this unusual view of the Grandstand, still closed for the winter, includes half a dozen horsemen in an early morning workout.

"Windsor and Uncle Mow"   1873

Uncle Mow G. (trainer? or owner?) in the sulky poses with Windsor, a handsome looking trotter. Mow also appears in an additional stereo in the same location with another trotter: Black Watch.

"Life Saving Station, Galilee, Monmouth Beach, N.J." 1874

This typical U.S. Life Saving Station of the period was located on the high part of the beach east of what is now Ocean Avenue.

"Pleasure R.R. Ocean Hotel, Long Branch, N.J." 1873

A children's railroad provided entertainment on the grounds of the Ocean Hotel (formerly the Continental). A billboard advertisement on the right proclaims "GEO. W. LAIRD'S BLOOM OF YOUTH."

G.W. Pach – Pach Bros.

The Pach Brothers, Gustavus W. and Gotthelf, established their first studio on the grounds of the Continental Hotel in Long Branch in 1867. By 1873 they had also opened a studio in nearby Ocean Grove. Their advertisements proclaimed "G. W. Pach: out of door groups, turnouts and equestran figures and stereoscopic views." At this time they were also well established in New York City. They were soon noted for the quality of their out of door work as well as their indoor portraits.

Pach Brothers produced more Monmouth County stereographs than the combined output of all the other stereographers of Monmouth County views. There are two basic reasons for the Pach Brothers' prolific production. First, their output spanned two of the most popular decades of the stereoscopic era. Secondly, they had studios both in Long Branch and Ocean Grove at a time when that part of the Jersey Shore was America's most popular resort area.

It is obvious, then, that Pach Brothers were in an enviable position to market their local stereo views. These three-dimensional photographs were an excellent souvenir of the Jersey Shore in a pre-postcard era. Hundreds of boarding houses, hotels, cottages and beach scenes as well as groups of delighted visitors in a summer holiday mood are preserved for all time on these delightful cards.

More than one stereo view of a subject was often taken at a single photo-session. Many of these "extra" or "secondary" views were also published...although frequently unnumbered and untitled.

From their New York Studio, Pach Brothers produced a variety of other interesting stereo views of and around New York City, as well as nearby colleges, Sing Sing, West Point, and Hudson River views.

Known as "Photographers to the Presidents" (from President Grant to President Nixon) the firm, after years of exceptional portrait work, ceased doing business in 1993.

A more detailed history of Pach Brothers can be found in "Those Innocent Years - 1898-1914 - Images of the Jersey Shore from the Pach Photographic Collection" by George H. Moss Jr. and Karen L. Schnitzspahn published by Ploughshare Press in 1993.

Published in 1868, J.H. Schenck's scarce "A Complete Descriptive Guide of Long Branch, N. J." carried this informative advertisement for G. W. Pach.

This imprint, from the back of a carte-de-visite, indicates the scope of Pach's business by 1880.

Pach's Ocean Grove Gallery was only open during the summer months. This June 5, 1875 advertisement from the Ocean Grove Record indicates the desire to photograph "everything of interest at the Grove" and includes a rare reference to their stereoscopic work.

Pach's Photograph Gallery, Long Branch, N.J.

In 1878 Pach's Gallery displayed many of their local stereo views in the Gallery's front window. The awning carried the words "Stereoscopic Views."

G. W. Pach's Photographic Wagon   1876

For advertising purposes Pach's Photographic Wagon was occasionally included in their stereographs as seen here in this Asbury Park view.

22. *"Bathing Scene at Long Branch, N. J."* 1870

> Low tide at the beach. In the foreground an advertisement for "Frank Leslie's Lady's Journal" is displayed on a bathhouse roof. Itchy, dark woolen bathing suits can be seen drying in the sun.

126. *"The Bluff and Beach. Long Branch, N.J."*

> A very popular seashore scene depicted by many renowned artists of the period including Winslow Homer. Homer, as early as 1868, often visited Long Branch.

LBU 604b Iron Pier, Long Branch, N.J.

Sitting on the beach in the shade of this new pier, summer visitors of 1879 watch with interest as the New York steamboat ADELAIDE slowly pulls along side with more holiday crowds bound for this Jersey resort.

LBU 603a Entrance to the Iron Pier, Long Branch, N.J.

Afternoon boardwalk strollers pause for the camera. Once the gate to the pier is open, the group will proceed to sit under the large canopy and enjoy the cool ocean breeze.

193. "Leland's Gun, Long Branch, N.J."   1873

Located on the bluff overlooking the Atlantic Ocean, this cannon, called "Old Monmouth," answered salutes of passing vessels as early as 1866. Leland's Ocean House (above) was then the Continental Hotel. This tradition continued into the early 1880's.

127. "Howland's Hotel," Long Branch, N.J.

Also on the bluff overlooking the ocean. Howland's Hotel was a favorite of many fine Philadelphia families including the Whartons and Biddles. Many guests were summer visitors for a number of decades...an indication that somebody was doing something right.

153. Mr. Woolman Stokes' Cottage, Long Branch, N.J.

Stokes was a Long Branch resident since 1850 and an owner and builder of a number of local hotels. In 1865 he erected this cottage..."with heaters, gas and other modern accessories to the convenience and comfort of the occupants. It is a double house, exceedingly commodious and well arranged, containing some twenty-one rooms."

132. "Hon. John McKeon and family" 1873

McKeon was a native New Yorker and prominent politician (a United States District Attorney and twice elected to Congress). G. W. Pach's camera has captured this pleasing portrait of the fashionably dressed McKeon family at their ocean view cottage, "Miramar," at the foot of Atlantic and Ocean Avenues, Long Branch.

119

175. "Lake Pathway, Ocean Grove, N.J."

Reverend Ellwood H. Stokes (left) and Alfred Cookman (white coat) and other members of the Ocean Grove Camp Meeting Association posed for this stereographic portrait prior to September 1871.

187. "Mrs. Stone's Tent," Ocean Grove, N.J.   1875

Tent life at Ocean Grove is still part of the Methodist Camp Meeting Association grounds today. Sea shells from the nearby ocean add a decorative touch to this summer portrait.

OGU 200 Tent Life at Ocean Grove, N.J.   1875

    A larger tent, complete with raised porch, is a fine background for this interesting group portrait.

OGU 210 Tent Life at Ocean Grove, N.J.   1875

    This relaxed group portrait also reveals hats and bonnets hanging inside on the left wall of the tent. In the background (right of center) a maid, holding a broom, smiles for the camera.

OGU 214 Memorial Vase Dedication Ceremony

This Memorial Vase was dedicated on July 31, 1875, the sixth anniversary of the first religious meeting held in Ocean Grove. Included with other members of the Camp Meeting Assocation is the Rev. E. H. Stokes (right).

OGU 226a Beach Meeting, Ocean Grove, N.J.

Ocean Grove Beach Meetings, held for many years, were extremely popular as documented by this July 27, 1876 view.

129. "River Scene at Red Bank," N.J.

This overall view of Red Bank's waterfront business section includes J. T. Allen's lumber yard (center) at the foot of Maple Avenue. The background includes the docks of J. Abbot Worthley, John W. Stout, J. A. Throckmorton and the Merchant's Steamboat Company. The paddle wheel steamboat *Sea Bird* is moored at the Wharf Avenue Dock.

149. "Shrewsbury" 1873

The three hundred year old Allen House is the property of the Monmouth County Historical Association and a worthy restoration for the enjoyment of future generations.

G. W. PACH/PACH BROS. STEREOGRAPHIC VIEWS

The following is a reference and study catalogue of G. W. Pach's Monmouth County, N. J., stereographic views.

The first section lists the NUMBERED views (1 through 275) as issued - not in the order they were photographed. The second section lists over 312 additional stereo cards of Pach's UNNUMBERED (and often untitled) views of Monmouth County.

Description of the Cards

1. Pach's first stereo views, produced ca. 1868, were issued on either yellow, green or, occasionally, on gray cards.

2. During 1870, as this early stock was depleted, the color was changed to red. Generally speaking, the yellow, green, gray and earliest red cards have no printed information on the face. For identification they have a label affixed to the back with Pach's name and New York City address (858 Broadway) and the card's title and number. There are at least seven different Long Branch labels and two different Ocean Grove labels. (G. W. Pach also produced a variety of stereo views of Princeton University, West Point, Sing Sing and New York City, but that is another story. By far the greatest number of Pach's stereographs are of Monmouth County).

3. The next major card change was to print Pach's name and address on the face of the card and to add the phrase "Title on Back" at the bottom right front corner. The identifying label was still placed on the back.

4. A still later change eliminated that label. Pach's name, address (studio locations) and the locale of the stereo view were printed on the face of the card i.e. "Long Branch Views." The number and very often the identifying title were both printed within the actual photograph. The earlier labels and even these newer card mounts were frequently mismatched: LONG BRANCH labels or cards were used for OCEAN GROVE or ASBURY PARK views and vice versa. In some instances the same card was reissued with a different title.

Section Two: Unnumbered and untitled views:

The final change was to issue cards without a title or numerical identification (but still with Pach's name and general location of the stereo view - i.e. "Scenes of Asbury Park and Ocean Grove"). While it is possible to identify most of these stereo views, there are still many that cannot be specifically identified and must remain little more than a "typical view" i.e. "Bathing Scene" or "Cottage Scene." Most dates given to Pach's stereo views are reasonable, but subject to correction. Manuscript dates found on the back of a card were often written at the time of purchase - not at the time the photograph was taken.

Pach's 858 Broadway, N.Y. address was used until 1878, when it was then changed to 841 Broadway. In all, there are more than forty variations of the information printed on the face of Pach's stereo cards. Many of Pach's most popular views (the Grant Cottage, for example) were reissued through the years. A view issued in 1870 might be found on five or six different card mounts and even reissued as late as 1882.

While the standard format of most of Pach's stereo cards are 3 3/8 x 6 7/8 inches, Pach did issue a few larger cards (cabinet size) which are 3 7/8 x 6 7/8 inches with gold lettering and maroon beveled edges.

G. W. Pach/Pach Bros. issued at least a thousand different stereographic views of Monmouth County, New Jersey, including Asbury Park, Ocean Grove, Long Branch, Oceanport, Monmouth Park Race Track, Red Bank, Sea Bright, Shrewsbury and views along the Navesink and Shrewsbury Rivers. Prominent individuals of the period were also photographed as well as newsworthy events. More than one stereograph of a subject was occasionally taken at a single photo-session. Many of these were also issued but usually without a number or title. Where possible, I have included these and similar views of the same subject adding a, b, or c to the original catalogue number. All other unnumbered and untitled cards are assigned a Moss Archives number: (Long Branch) = "LBU -" ; (Ocean Grove) = "OGU -" or (Asbury Park) APU -".

Interestingly, it appears almost fifty of Pach's Monmouth County views were re-issued (or pirated) by other stereo publishers.

There are still many Monmouth County stereographs by G. W. Pach yet to be documented. There are obvious gaps in the Pach Catalogue and, I am sure, another 200 or so views without numbers or titles exist in other collections. Any additions would be a welcome and valuable contribution to this ongoing project.

PACH MONMOUTH COUNTY NUMBERED VIEWS FOUND ON DIFFERENT COLORED CARDS

YELLOW CARDS:		GREEN CARDS:	GREY CARDS:
5 L	86 M	28 L	U57b L
14 L	88 L (1870)	44 L	127b L
22 L	99 L	113 L	
23 1/2		118 L	
37 L		126 L	
53 M			
59 L			
71 L			

The following are RED CARDS:

LABEL ONLY on back:		"TITLE ON BACK" and LABEL:		Number in Photo. No LABEL:		Handwritten Title on back. No LABEL	
4	196a	1	243	5	174	1	239
5	197	24	254	7	175	2	242
6	231	25	255	11	180	3	
7	261	48		20	187	9	
9		52		22	193	12	
13		56		23 1/2	197	20	
15		59		29	200	23 1/2	
20		65		30	206	26	
21		78		43	212	41	
26		88	(1870)	44	232	49	
27		101b		47	241	55	
30		103		52	242	57	
35		111		53	248	59a	
40		120		58	251	59b	
48		124		59	252	60	
49		128		63	254	81a	
50		129		76	255	81b	
54		132		78		85	
59		138		88	(1870)	88	(1870)
60		140		91		100b	
64		141		94		101a	
69		146		100		117a	
74		168		110		125	
77		169		117		127a	
88	(1870)	175		118		144	
91		193		127		145	
96		196		136		155	
99		208		137		171	
103		211		139		196b	
104		213		142		196c	
117		226		144		197	
122		228		155		200a	
126		231		158		226	
133		238		171		228a	

PACH CATALOG

Section One: Numbered Views

Explanations:

Title and/or number taken from either LABEL [L], PHOTOGRAPH [P] or contemporary MANUSCRIPT [M].

LB = Long Branch   OALB = Ocean Avenue, Long Branch
AP = Asbury Park   OG = Ocean Grove

1L	"Sea Side Chapel" Chelsea and Ocean Avenues, LB
2M	"Ocean Hotel Spa" on Bluff, OALB
3M	"Franklin House"
4L	"Bathing Scene" LB
5P	"Bathing Scene" LB
6L	"Crabbing at Sea Bright" - same photo-session as #103
7L	"Our Spitz" LB
8L	"Three Cottages Facing Wesley Lake," OG
9L	"Metropolitan Hotel" OALB
10	
11P	"Green's Pond" now Takanassee Lake
12M	"Wesley Lake" OG
13L	"Ocean Hotel Promenade" (porch) OALB
14L	"Steamboat Helen at Red Bank N.J."

14. "Steamboat HELEN at Red Bank, N. J."

A nice calm view of the Navesink River (1870) and of the paddle wheel steamer *Helen*, dockside at Red Bank.

15L	"J. K. Heyward Cottage" Lake & New Jersey Aves., OG
16	
17	
18P	"View in Hoey's Park" LB
19	
20L	"Altar Grounds" OG
21L	"Bathing Scene" LB
22L	"Bathing Scene" LB reissued on LITTLETON #1373
23 1/2P	"View in Hoey's Park" LB Same photo-session as #94
24L	"Mr. Stokes Cottage" LB Wardell Ave. near Chelsea
25L	"Childs Cottage" LB
26M	"Steven's Boat, Sea Bright"
27L	"J. H. Thornley Cottage" OG Lake Ave near Wesley Place
28L	"Arlington House" OALB
29P	"Atlantic Ocean"
30L	"View of the Atlantic Ocean" LB
31	
32	
33	
34L	"Jos B. Yard's Cottage" OG
35L	"D. P. Foist Cottage" OG
36	
37L	"Rev. G. Hughes Cottage" OG
38	
39L	"Coleman Cottage" OG
40M	"Congressman N. Terry's Cottage" LB
41M	"The Atlantic Ocean" – same photo-session as #30L
42M	"View of Atlantic Ocean" same photo-session as #30L
43P	"Jeremiah Curtis Cottage" LB
44L	"View From Bluff" OALB
44P	"Bathing Scene" LB – same negative as above
45	
46	
47P	"A Canine Group"
48L	"Edwin Booth's Cottage" LB – also LITTLETON #1279
49L	"J. W. Wallack & Friends" LB
50L	"Hon. Thomas Murphy Cottage" LB
51	
52L	"Chelsea Ave. LB
53Ma	"Ocean View" LB
53Pb	"Atlantic Ocean" same negative as above.
54L	"Street Scene (at river) Red Bank, N.J."
55M	"View of Atlantic Ocean"
56L	"Boat Scene at Sea Bright"
57L	"Flynn's Pleasure Bay Dock"
58P	"View of Atlantic Ocean"
59La	"West End Hotel" LB
59Mb	"West End Hotel" rt to lft with Hotel carriage
59Mc	"West End Hotel" lft to rt with four small carriages

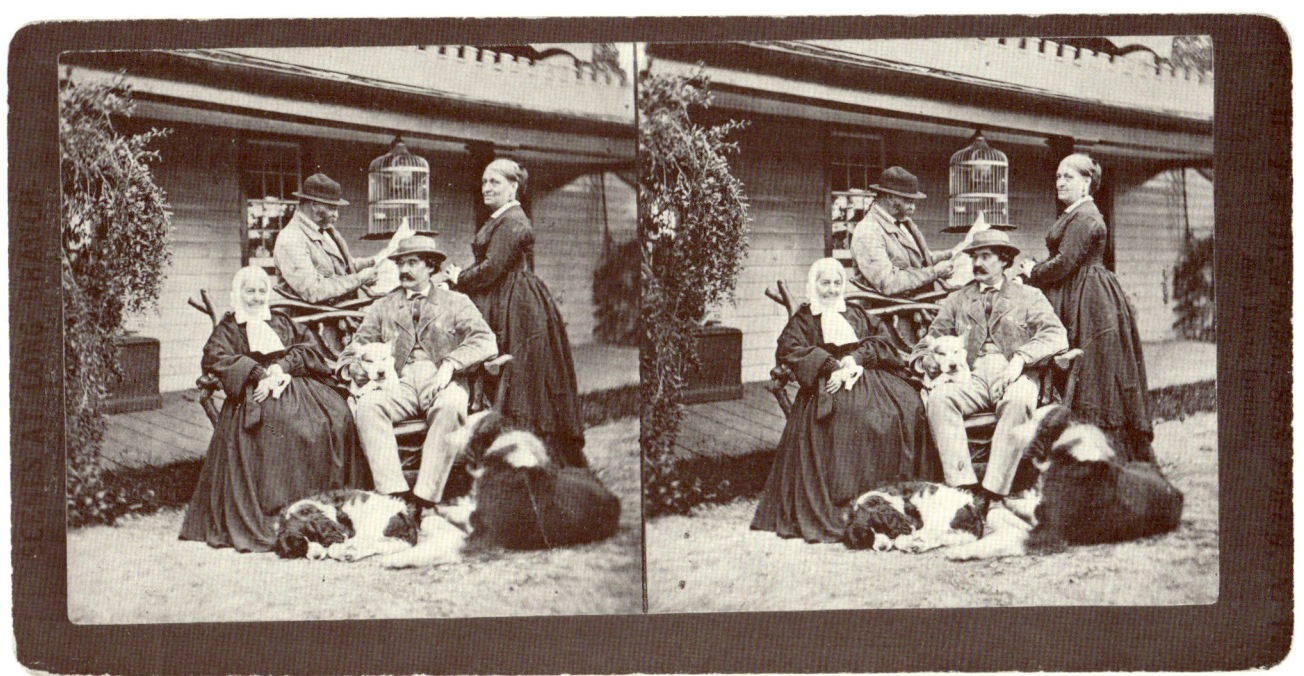

49 "J.W. Wallack and friends" 1870

A noted actor in his time, J. W. Wallack posed with friends at "Hopefield", one of his two cottages at Long Branch. This photo-session is most interesting because at least three different portraits were taken by G. W. Pach at this sitting. Pach's first choice became stereo view #49. A second negative – different, but similar in pose – was either sold or pirated and appears on all of the following four stereo cards:

        A - "AMERICAN VIEWS   LONG BRANCH, N. J.
        James W. Wallack & Family"   (red card-gray back)

        B - "LONG BRANCH
        James W. Wallack & Family"   (red card)

        C - "NEW YORK CITY VIEWS   (green card)
        James W. Wallack & Family"

        D - "American Scenery   American Scenery   (yellow card)
        James W. Wallack and Family at Long Branch, N.J."

Imprint on back of the above card: "Published by L. L. Tarbell, Jr..."
(see following page)
"James W. Wallack and Family at Long Branch, N.J."

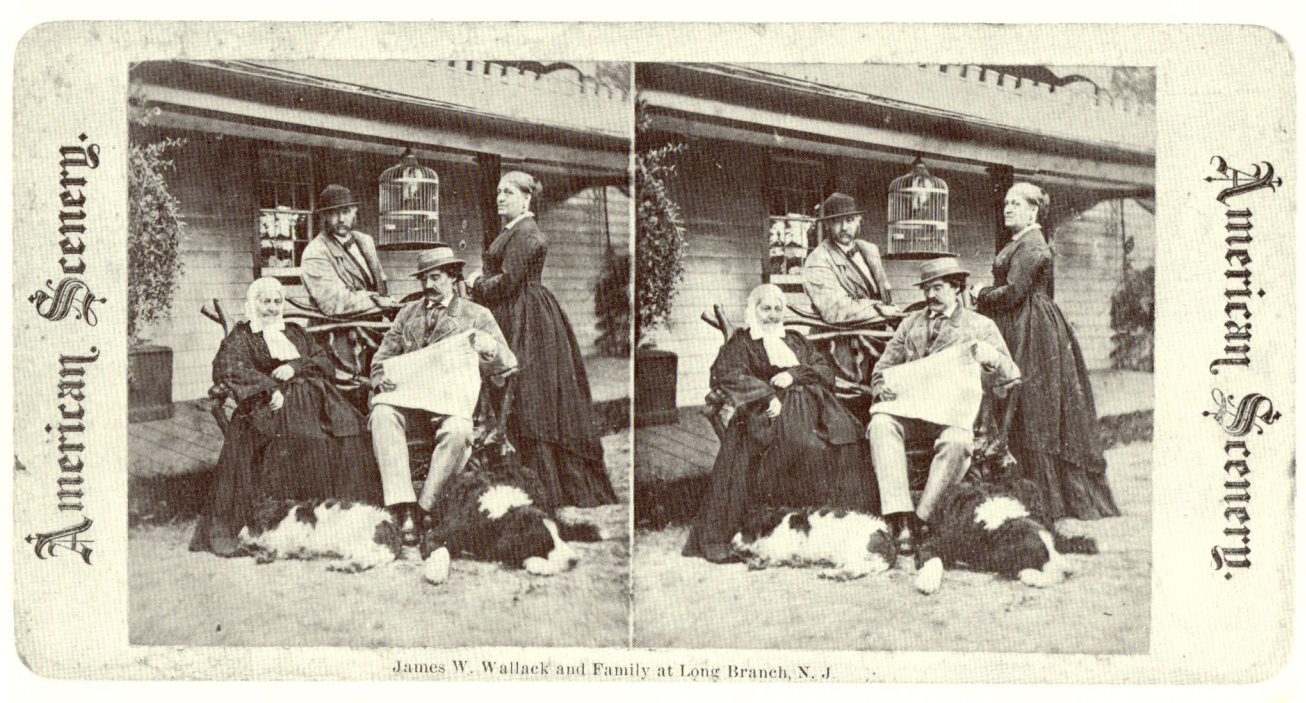

"James W. Wallack and Family at Long Branch, N.J."
"American Scenery – American Scenery" (yellow card)

Imprint on back of the above card

L. L. Tarbell, Jr., Publisher.
Marlboro, Mass.

"G.W. Pach, 858 B'dway. N.Y." "Long Branch. & Ocean Grove, N.J."

Pach's stereo card #49 refers to "J. W. Wallack & FRIENDS" while all the other cards refer to "J. W. Wallack and FAMILY." A third negative produced from this same photo-session (slightly different pose and not stereographic) was used by G. W. Pach for the above striking enlargement. The names written on the reverse of this original print are: "Mrs. J. W. Wallack Jr., J. W. Wallack Jr. (seated) and Dr. Blake and Mrs W. R. Blake."

60M	"(John F.) Chamberlin's Club House" later Phil Daly's
61	
62	
63P	"Billy Goats" in front of Ocean Hotel OALB
64L	"Widow Cookman's Cottage" OG Lake Avenue between Wesley Place and Pilgrim Pathway
65L	"Croquet Group" OALB
66	
67	
68	
69L	"Bathing Scene" OG
70	
71L	"Monmouth Park - on the Home Stretch" – same photo-session as # 76 – also LITTLETON #1272
72	
73	
74L	"Green's Pond" (Takanassee Lake)
75L	"View of Ocean From Bluff"
76L	"Monmouth Park" – same photo-session as #71
77L	"Rev. John Treskip's Cottage OG
78La	"Boat Scene at Sea Bright same photo-session as #26
78Pb	"Stephen's Boat, Sea Bright" same as above
79	
80	
81Pa	"United States Hotel" OALB
81b	"United States Hotel" OALB – different view
81c	"United States Hotel" OALB – different view
82	
83	
84	
85M	"Ocean Ave from Green's Pond" (Takanassee Lake)
86L	"Grandstand Monmouth Park" LB
87	
88	There are actually six, almost identical, Pach negatives of the Grant Cottage. Taken over a period of more than a year, they were ALL issued as #88! I have designated the six similar views: #88 A through #88 F)
88A L	"Grant's Cottage"
88B L	"Grant's Cottage"
88C L,P,M	"Grant's Cottage"
	#88A, 88B and 88C taken at same photo-session
88D M	"Grant's Cottage"
88E M	"Grant's Cottage"
	#88D and 88E taken at later photo-session
88F M	"Grant's Cottage"
	#88F taken at still another photo-session.

88. *President Grant's Cottage, Elberon, N.J.* 1870

Completed in June of 1867, and originally the residence of Howard Potter, this cottage was a gift to President Ulysses S. Grant in 1869. Grant summered at the Jersey Shore for over a decade. This popular card (#88) was in demand for over a dozen years.

PRESIDENT GRANT'S COTTAGE AT LONG BRANCH.—[Phot. by E. W. Pach.]

Before it was possible to reproduce photographs in newspapers and magazines, illustrations were usually wood engravings. In his studio and unable to actually visit a scene, an artist often used a photograph of his subject to create his work. The above August 13, 1870 wood engraving from Harper's Weekly credits Pach's photo as the source for this illustration.

89L	"Ocean Avenue North from Green's Pond"
90P	"School House in Red Bank" - Mechanic Street
91L	"Entrance to Monmouth Park"
91Pb	Shift in printing shows photographer's box of film
92	
93	
94P	"View in Hoey's Park" same photo-session as # 23 1/2
95	
96L	"Hoey's Park" LB
97	
98	
99L	"Cows at Green's Pond" LB (Lake Takanassee)
100Pa	"Central Hotel" OALB (H.C. Shoemaker, Prop) opened 1873-74 under Shoemaker
100Mb	Central Hotel OALB Different view. (Vollmer & Jauss)
101Ma	Ocean Hotel Dining Room OALB
101Mc	Ocean Hotel Dining Room OALB
101Mb	Ocean Hotel Dining Room OALB # 61 ?
102	
103L	"Crabbing Scene"
104L	"View of the Atlantic Ocean" from LB
105	
106	
107	View of Pleasure Bay

90. "School House in Red Bank," N.J.

Still standing, although with a number of structural additions, this former school building located at Mechanic Street is easily identified.

108	
109	
110P	"Bathing Scene"
111L	"View of the Atlantic Ocean" from LB
112	
113L	"On the Race" Monmouth Park
114	
115	Cottage LB
116	
117La	"Mansion House" OALB
117Pb	"Mansion House" OALB
117c	"Mansion House" OALB same photo-session as above
118La	"Pedestrian Path to Ocean Hotel" OALB
118Pb	"Path to Ocean Hotel" OALB
119L	Sycamore Ave., Shrewsbury NYHS
120L	Wesley Lake. Four rowboats
121	Sea Bright from Rumson
122L	Similar. Same photo-session as above
123	
124L	"Miss Maggie Mitchell's Cottage"
125M	"George W. Curtis' Cottage" West End, LB
126La	"Bluff and Beach View" LB
126Lb	"The Bluff and Beach" LB same view
127Pa	"Howland's Hotel" OALB
127Mb	"Howland's Hotel" OALB diff view
127Lc	"Howland's Hotel" OALB (GREY card)
128L	"Iauch's Hotel" OALB
129L	"River Scene at Red Bank near Long Branch"
130	
131L	"Lester Wallack's Cottage" LB
132L	"Hon. John McKeon and Family" OALB
133L	"View of the Atlantic Ocean from Long Branch"
134	
135	
136P	"View in Hoey's Park" LB boy at rustic gate
137P	"Atlantic Ocean"
138L	"Bathing Scene at Long Branch"
139P	"View in Hoey's Park" LB
140L	"West End Parlour" LB
141La	"The Beach & Bluff"
141Lb	"The Beach at Long Branch" same as above
142P	"Bathing Scene" LB
143	
144Pa	"The Surf" LB
144Ma	"Bathing Scene" LB same as above
145M	Ocean Scene - three sailing vessels LB
146L	"View of the Atlantic Ocean from Long Branch"
147L	"Shrewsbury" (stable at left)

148	
149L	"Shrewsbury"(Allen House)
150	
151	
152	
153P	Rev. E. H. Stokes and Cottage OG
154	Wesley Lake OG
155P	Boat Scene - Wesley Lake OG
156	
157	
158P	Boat Scene OG same photo-session as #155
159	
160	
161	
162	
163	Rev E. H. Stokes First Cottage OG
164L	Trenton House OG
165	Howland House
166	
167	
168L	"Lawrence Boarding House" OG
169L	"Post Office" OG
170P	Dr. Karsner's Tent
171P	"Pilgrim's Pathway" OG
172	
173L	Wesley Lake OG
174P	Four Tents OG
175P	"Lake Pathway" OG (Tents, Rev. Stokes & Cookman)
176L	"Lawrence Boarding House" OG
177L	Wesley Lake OG
178	
179	
180P	"Pilgrim's Pathway"
181	
182	
183P	Osborn Cottage
184P	Mrs. Stone's Tent
185	
186	
187P	"Mrs. Stone's Tent"
188	
189	
190	
191	
193L	"Leland's Gun" OALB
193P	"Leland's Gun" OALB
194	

155. "Boat Scene, Wesley Lake, Ocean Grove, N.J."

Boating was extremely popular more than a century ago. Statistics show there were 530 rowboats on Wesley Lake in 1877. Nearby undeveloped Fletcher Lake had only 35 boats that year.

This carte-de-visite was made from one of the stereographic negatives used to print the above boat scene in 1872. Pach issued a few other cartes-de-visite (including Monmouth Park Grandstand) using one negative from the stereographic pair.

195	
196La	"Ocean Hotel" OALB
196Lb	"Ocean Hotel" OALB - same photo-session
196Mc	"Ocean Hotel" OALB - different photo-session
196Md	Ocean Hotel and Coach closeup OALB
196Me	"Ocean Hotel" OALB entire hotel
197L	"Hoey's Cottage and Grounds"
197Pa	"View in Hoey's Park" same view
198Ma	"View in Hoey's Park" same view as #197
199	
200Pa	"View of Hoey's Cottage" with two gardeners
200Mb	"Hollywood, residence of Mr. John Hoey" different view
201	"Monmouth Park Club House"
202	
203	
204	Sol Cohen's Cottage LB
205	
206P	"Statue of Mercury in Hoey's Park"
207	Boy on Pony in Hoey's Park
208La	"Fountain at Hoey's Park"
208Pb	"Fountain in Hoey's Park"
209L	Birds eye view. Carriage in foreground
210	Hoey's Woods
211L	"Secy Robeson's Cottage" LB (G M Robeson? Surf Road)
212P	"Ocean Pathway" OG
213L	"Terry's (Torry's) Cottage" LB
214	
215	
216	
217	
218	
219	
220	Bathing Scene OG
221	
222	
223	
224	
225L	Lt. Reed Cottage OG
226L	"Park Hall, Asbury Park"
227	
228La	"Park Hall" (Steinbach, AP)
228Mb	Steinbach Block
229	
230	
231L	"Mt. Pisga Ave" OG
232P	Wesley Lake" OG
233	Brown's Cottage OG

201. *"Monmouth Park Club House"*   1870

Opening day at Monmouth Park was on July 30, 1870. A major attraction at the shore for both men and women. Dozens of fashionably dressed ladies crowd the upper porch of the Club House.

228. *"Park Hall"*   1874

An early view of Asbury Park's "Branch Store of Steinbach Bros – East Long Branch, N.J."

234	
235	Wesley Lake
236	
237	
238L	"Main Ave"
239M	"Mr. Beegle's Cottage" OG
240	
241P	"Forsch's Pavilion" foot of Main Ave
242P	"Forsch's Pavilion" same photo-session as #241
243L	"Central Ocean Pathway" OG
244	
245	Hayward Cottage
246	North Ocean Pathway OG
247	Wesley Lake OG
248Pa	"Wesley Lake" OG
248Mb	Wesley Lake. OG Closeup of Rev Stokes.
249	
250L	Hayward's Cottage OG
251Pa	"View of Asbury Park" over Wesley Lake
252Pb	"View of Asbury Park" same photo-session as #251
253	
254La	"View of Asb. Park" rowboat IDA MAY
254Pb	Same as above
255La	"View of Asbury Park" rowboat IDA MAY
255Pb	"View of Asbury Park" same photo-session as #254
256	
257	
258	
259M	Fairy Island Gazebo OG
260	
261L	"Wesley Lake"
262	
263	Central Avenue from Main
264	
265L	Hostetters Cottage
266	
267	Beach Meeting
268	
269	Beach Meeting
270	
271	
272	
273	Park Hall AP
274	
275	

Section Two: Unnumbered and Untitled Views

Unnumbered and untitled identifiable Asbury Park views by Pach Brothers. "APU-" is Moss Archives numbering system.

BUILDINGS, ASBURY PARK

APU 1	Bevan House
APU 2	Cahill House
APU 3	Carlton
APU 4	Coleman House - Surrey and wagon in foreground
APU 5	Crescent House
APU 6a	Grand Avenue House - Distant view
APU 6b	Grand Avenue House - Medium view
APU 6c	Grand Avenue House - Close-up
APU 7a	Lakeview House
APU 7b	Lakeview House
APU 8	The Madison
APU 9a	Ocean View House
APU 9b	Ocean View House - Close-up
APU 10a	Sea Rest. "Woman's Christian Asc. of Asbury Park"
APU 10b	"Asbury Park Ladies Christian Asc. Home"
APU 10c	"Asbury Park Ladies Christian Asc. Home"

APU 9b Ocean View House, Asbury Park, N.J.   1876

This delightful glimpse of the Ocean View House with its many visitors captures a relaxed moment in an otherwise busy summer day.

APU 11a	Working Girl's Home - opening 1874
APU 11b	Working Girl's Home same photo session
APU 12	Trinity Church. Asbury & Grand Aves. 1879
APU 13	Cooper's Cottage. 1877
APU 14	Two story cottage and "Bradley & Smith, Brushes" wagon
APU 15	Evelesis (sp?) Cottage 1872
APU 16	-oche Cottage

SUNSET LAKE VIEWS, ASBURY PARK

APU 100	Small crowd at Sunset Lake. + "Grand Ave. Ferry" and Foot Bridge
APU 101	Two men in rowboat with two women rowing – near Ferry
APU 102	Group in Ferry and seven in rowboat LULU WIDDY
APU 103	Two couples in "Grand Ave. Ferry"
APU 104	View of foot bridge to "Ice Cream Garden"
APU 105a	Close-up of group on foot bridge
APU 105b	Close-up of another group on foot bridge
APU 106a	Early close-up of refreshment stand
APU 106b	Later close-up of refreshment stand
APU 107	Two rowboats – three women in one and two men in the other
APU 108	Seven people in rowboat at shore. Man sitting on shore
APU 109	Couple in rowboat. Two youngsters in background 1883
APU 110	Couple in rowboat, ashore and two men in rowboat ashore 1885
APU 111	St. John's Island (pic-nic area and boat house) Sunset Lake

WESLEY LAKE VIEWS, ASBURY PARK

APU 112	Asbury Park Pilot - bridge and rowboats 1875
APU 113	Asbury Park Inlet 1875 similar to below
APU 114	Wesley Lake boats and lake shore and trees
APU 115	Wesley Lake view of Ocean Grove from Lake View House?

BEACH and BATHING SCENES, ASBURY PARK

APU 200	Group of bathers in ankle deep water
APU 201	Seated group on beach watching bathers 1883
APU 202	Crowded beach and bathers. Umbrella in foreground
APU 203	Crowded beach and bathers at foot of Cahill House avenue
APU 204	On the beach at Asbury Park Pavilion

APU 103 Grand Avenue Ferry, Sunset Lake, Asbury Park, N.J.   1876

A rustic resting place while waiting for the ferry ride to the striped refreshment stand in mid-lake.

APU 106b Refreshment Stand, Sunset Lake, Asbury Park, N.J.   1876

"Segars" for the gentlemen and F. Kurrus' rich and creamy ice cream for the ladies were the special attractions at this stand.

Identifiable Ocean Grove Cards

Unnumbered and untitled identifiable Ocean Grove views by Pach Brothers. "OGU series" is Moss Archives numbering system. Similar views of subject have identical number plus a, b or c.

HOTELS, BOARDING HOUSES, PRIVATE COTTAGES:

OGU 1	Aldine House. 28 Main Avenue
OGU 2a	The Arlington. Pilgrim Pathway close-up
OGU 2b	The Arlington
OGU 3a	Centennial House. 63 Main Avenue close-up
OGU 3b	Centennial House
OGU 4	Central Cottage earlier view of Central House
OGU 5	Central House. 15 Main Avenue
OGU 6	N. T. Childs Cottage
OGU 7	Columbia Cottage
OGU 8	J. G. Cooper Cottage. Heck Avenue
OGU 9	Rev. J. R. Daniels Cottage
OGU 10	Drew Cottage
OGU 11	Fielder Cottage
OGU 12	Friendship Cottage

OGU 2b The Arlington Hotel, Ocean Grove, N.J.

This pioneer hotel, photographed in 1878, had a capacity of three hundred occupants and served the community for almost a hundred years.

OGU 13	Germantown House. Central and Heck Avenues
OGU 14	Grace Cottage. 47 Webb Avenue
OGU 15a	Granite State Cottage
OGU 15b	Granite State Cottage
OGU 15c	Granite State Cottage later view
OGU 16	Grove Cottage. Main and Lawrence Avenues
OGU 17a	Howland House. 65 Mt. Tabor Way close-up
OGU 17b	Howland House close-up
OGU 17c	Howland House
OGU 18a	Johnson House
OGU 18b	Johnson House
OGU 18c	Johnson House close-up
OGU 19	Laurel Cottage
OGU 20a	Lawrence House. 43 Main Avenue
OGU 20b	Lawrence House close-up
OGU 20c	Lawrence House close-up
OGU 21	Martin Cottage
OGU 22	Mt. Tabor Cottage. Mt. Tabor Way near Delaware Ave.
OGU 23	Norman Cottage. 30 Bath Avenue
OGU 24	Ocean Avenue House. 17 Ocean Avenue
OGU 25	Ocean Front. 1 Main Avenue
OGU 26	Ocean Hall
OGU 27	Olive House. 19 Heck Avenue
OGU 28a	Osborn House. Central and Pitman Avenues
OGU 28b	Osborn House 1879
OGU 29a	Pitman House. 24 Pitman Avenue
OGU 29b	Pitman House
OGU 30a	Sheldon House
OGU 30b	Sheldon House
OGU 31	Spray View House. Ocean and Spray View Avenues
OGU 32	Stark's Cottage
OGU 33	Thorne's Cottage/Thorne's Dining Rooms
OGU 34a	Tower Cottage close-up
OGU 34b	Tower Cottage
OGU 35	Cowell House (Banner across porch)
OGU 36	Bird's-eye view of Main Avenue
OGU 37	Bird's-eye view of Central Avenue
OGU 38	Main Avenue and the Post Office from Central Avenue
OGU39	Bird's-eye view of OG
OGU 40	Bird's-eye view of OG
OGU 41	Bird's-eye view of OG
OGU 42	Bird's-eye view of OG
OGU 43	Block House. Central and Pitman Avenues
OGU 44	St. Pauls M. E. Church 1876
OGU 45	Tabernacle (Tent) 1875
OGU 46	Tabernacle 1877
OGU 47a	Sunday School
OGU 47b	Sunday School
OGU 48	Second Auditorium 1875

OGU 49	Third Auditorium 1876
OGU 50	Third Auditorium 1876 view from Altar
OGU 51	Large group dining under tents
OGU 52	Small group dining in woods
OGU 53	Large crowd attending outdoor meeting
OGU 54	Ocean Pathway
OGU 55	Ocean Pathway with group of 6 people
OGU 56	Distant view of Ocean Pathway
OGU 57	Close-up of Ocean Pathway houses
OGU 58	Beersheba's Well from cottage second story
OGU 59	Croquet game in wooded park
OGU 99	View of Fletcher Lake
FAIRY ISLE AREA of WESLEY LAKE:	
OGU 100	Distant easterly view of Fairy Island before bridge
OGU 101	Distant easterly view of rowboats and Fairy Island
OGU 102	Similar scene - different rowboats
OGU 103	Two women on bridge to Fairy Island
OGU 104a	Closeup of boats and bridge to Fairy Island
OGU 104b	Similar view. Same photo session as above
OGU 105	Two crowded rowboats. Large group on bridge

Auditorium, Ocean Grove, N.J. July 1876

Occupied for the first time on July 2, 1876, this auditorium was decorated with flags and bunting for the United States Centennial Celebration.

OGU 106	Four crowded rowboats. Large group on bridge and Island
OGU 107	Closeup of bridge and one boat
OGU 108	Distant eastern view from bridge. Three boats
OGU 109	Western view of bridge, Fairy Island and six rowboats
OGU 110	Western view. Closeup of bridge. Small crowd and one rowboat

GENERAL VIEWS AROUND WESLEY LAKE:

OGU 111	Naptha Launch at dock
OGU 112	Canopied rowboat
OGU 113	Shore, lake and boats. (looking east.) YELLOW CARD and label
OGU 113	Shore, lake and boats. (looking east.) RED CARD and label
OGU 114	Similar but closer view RED CARD and label
OGU 115	Lake shore. Small Crowd. Rev. Stokes
OGU 116	Looking west over Fairy Island towards Lake View House
OGU 117a	View over mid-lake towards Asbury Park
OGU 117b	Similar view - same photo session
OGU 118	Close-up of numerous rowboats at lake shore
OGU 119	Similar view
OGU 120	Closeup of crowded boats at shore
OGU 121	View from porch looking east over entire Lake
OGU 122	Closer view of similar scene
OGU 123	Even closer view of similar scene
OGU 124	Lake Avenue looking east
OGU 125	Similar view but of entire lake
OGU 126	Close-up along Lake Avenue. Cottages, three women and Lake
OGU 127	View from Asbury Park of P. H. Fowler, Rev. H. M. Sanders and E.. Rogers Ocean Grove Cottages
OGU 128	Close-up of Fowler Cottage
OGU 129a	Close-up of Rev. Sanders' Cottage
OGU 129b	Similar view
OGU 129c	Similar view
OGU 130	Three cottages on Ocean Grove shore
OGU 131	Eastern Point of Wesley Lake at Ocean
OGU 132	Same photo session 1874
OGU 133	Children in ocean at east end of Wesley Lake
OGU 134	Wesley Lake from Asbury Park. Crowded boat at shore 1874
OGU 135	Two boats in Wesley Lake near dock

TENT LIFE and RELIGIOUS ACTIVITIES

OGU 200	Group of 9 in front of tent. Pair of oars against tree
OGU 201	Four ladies at tent. Mrs. Grant ? dressed in white
OGU 202	Close-up of Vase by the Tabernacle
OGU 203	"Pioneer Women Vase" (in front of two tents.)
OGU 204	Janitor's Office tent
OGU 205	Large group in front of row of tents

OGU 206	View inside of tent. Five women and boy in photo
OGU 207	Family portrait of seven seated in tent
OGU 208	Closed tent. Seven people and boy with pair of oars
OGU 209	"Mrs. James E. Terry, Mrs. Marcus B. Taylor, Miss Mary Taylor, Miss Maggie Morford, Lester Terry, Jacob Willse nephew of Mary Taylor" in fron of tent
OGU 210	Portrait of eleven at tent including a maid or cook.
OGU 211	Bethany. Orderly row of tents
OGU 212	Howland Avenue. Rows of tents and many families
OGU 213	Tents near small embankment at edge of forrest
OGU 214	Memorial Vase dedication, 1875. Rev. Stokes at right
OGU 215	Crowd scene at dedication
OGU 225a	Beach Meeting 1875
OGU 225b	Same photo session. Different angle
OGU 226a	Beach Meeting 1876
OGU 226b	Same photo session
OGU 227a	Beach Meeting 1883
OGU 227b	Same photo session
OGU 228	Beach Meeting similar to 227a/b
OGU 229a	Model of Jerusalem 1881
OGU 229b	Similar view
OGU 229c	Similar view
OGU 229d	Similar view
OGU 230	Large crowd - some seated - toy wagon 6 small children
OGU 231	Large crowd standing
OGU 232	Very large crowd, sitting and standing. A few in bathing suits
OGU 233	Large crowd. Typical Beach Meeting scene
OGU 234	Group of 30 all looking to right off camera
OGU 235	Formal crowd. Girl on white donkey in center
OGU 236	Large crowd. Children in foreground. Picnic basket at right
OGU 237	Large crowd. Typical Beach Meeting scene
OGU 238	Very large crowd. Typical Beach Meeting scene
OGU 239	Smaller crowd. A few in bathing suits seated on beach

BATHING and BEACH SCENES:

OGU 300	Group of 13 in bathing suits at water's edge (9 seated)
OGU 301a	Eleven children in shallow surf. Some holding bathing rope
OGU 301b	Same photo session. 3 young adults and bathing master
OGU 302	Group of 20 holding bathing rope. Wave breaking.
OGU 303	Close-up of many people in surf
OGU 304	Group of 13 youngsters in ankle deep surf
OGU 305	Crowded surf scene. Most facing camera
OGU 306	Group facing camera seated and standing in ankle deep water
OGU 309	Group of 14 wading in waste deep water
OGU 310	Group of 18 in bathing suits standing and sitting on beach
OGU 311	Beach group. Some dressed in bathing suits wading in water

OGU 312	Beach Group. Bath Houses in background
OGU 313	Very large crowd. Appears to be a Beach Meeting
OGU 314	Large group sitting and standing on beach
OGU 315	Another large group sitting and standing on beach
OGU 316	Group of forty. Flag flying with what appears to be number 38
OGU 317	Small group sitting and kneeling on beach

The following are unidentified Ocean Grove views. In most instances there are many individuals in the photo representing boarders, guests, family or friends.

OGU 400	Group close-up of porch of two story hotel
OGU 401	Close-up of three story boarding house - sign unreadable
OGU 402	Front view of two story boarding house - sign unreadable
OGU 403	Front view of four story boarding house
OGU 404	Large hotel - sign unreadable
OGU 405	Front view of large four story boarding house
OGU 406	Three story boarding house + seven boatmen with oars
OGU 407a	Twin cottages
OGU 407b	One of the twin cottages
OGU 408	Very small cottage. Group includes man with oar
OGU 409	Small two story (joined) twin cottages
OGU 410	Small two story cottage. Boy with high wheel bicycle
OGU 411	Two story cottage near Wesley Lake. Carriage and two horses
OGU 412	Two story cottage. Man in chair with daughter
OGU 413	Small Cottage. Woman with fan, man seated on porch
OGU 414	Two and a half story cottage # 389 -
OGU 415	Small two story cottage
OGU 416	Two and a half story cottage with wire fence
OGU 417	Two and a half story house with small white fence
OGU 418	Two and a half story cottage with bay window (Wesley Lake?)
OGU 419	Row of large Houses (near Wesley Lake?)
OGU 420	Row of cottages
OGU 421	Two story cottage (near Wesley Lake?)
OGU 422	Two and a half story cottage with bay window (not OGU 418)
OGU 423	Long two story building with awnings on side. Stores?
OGU 424	Two small stores (one is - Market)
OGU 425	Small two story building with sign on tree "Malcolm"

LBU 600c "Stranded Vessel at Long Branch, N.J."

The *Allie Rickman,* a three masted schooner out of Boston, ran into foul weather in July of 1874 and ended up high and dry on the beach at Long Branch.

LBU 602 "Wreck of the RUSLAND"

A victim of a winter storm on March 17, 1877, the Red Star Line steamer *Rusland* lies broken in two after striking the hull of a sunken vessel about 200 yards off Takanassee Beach (opposite the San Alfonso Retreat) at Long Branch.

Unnumbered identifiable Long Branch views by Pach Brothers.

"LBU - " is Moss Archives numbering system.

LBU 500 series are views of Frederick Hoey's residence and "Hollywood," Hoey's renowned estate and "Park."

LBU 500a	Distant view of Hoey's house and grounds and 1 man
LBU 500b	Similar view - no man. (Littleton # 1275)
LBU 500c	Hoey's house in distance. Two men in path.
LBU 500d	Side view of Hoey's porch
LBU 501a	Large two-tiered fountain
LBU 501b	Medium view of fountain
LBU 501c	Elevated view of fountain and grounds
LBU 501d	Similar view with two couples
LBU 502	Smaller three-tiered fountain and two people
LBU 503	Statue of four children playing with ostrich
LBU 504	Statue of two children playing with ostrich
LBU 505	Nude male warrior with sword and shield
LBU 505	Male "God" with cloak on large pedestal
LBU 507	Statue of fight between lioness, warrior and dog
LBU 508	Statue of young boy fighting lion
LBU 509	Lion, Lioness and two cubs
LBU 510	Large lion
LBU 511	Statue of cat with hat in paw
LBU 512	Statue of large boar
LBU 513a	Large stag on pedestal. Hoey's house in distance
LBU 513b	Same card cabinet size "Hollywood, Long Branch"
LBU 514	Similar, but different statue
LBU 515	Standing statue of stag. Hothouse in distance
LBU 516	Similar, but different statue
LBU 517	Tree lined street in Hoey's Garden
LBU 518	Forrest of slender trees. Hoey's Garden

Some of the following Long Branch cards (in particular generic beach and ocean views) were also issued as "Scenes at Ocean Grove and Asbury Park."

LBU 600a	Stranding of the "Allie Rickman" July 1874
LBU 600b	different view - same photo session
LBU 600c	different view - same photo session
LBU 601	Stranding of the "L'Amerique" Jan. 7, 1877
LBU 602	Wreck of the "Rusland" March 18, 1877
LBU 603a	Boardwalk and people at entrance to the Ocean Pier
LBU 603b	People seated under canopy of Ocean Pier
LBU 604a	South side of Ocean Pier from boardwalk
LBU 604b	Same view but with Steamer "Adelaide"
LBU 604c	Similar view taken minutes later
LBU 605a	North side of Ocean Pier and "Plymouth Rock"

LBU 605b	Taken minutes after 605a (LITTLETON # 1334)
LBU 605c	Similar view taken minutes after 605b
LBU 606	"President Grant at his Cottage by the Sea" 1872
LBU 607	Beach and Bluff - looking north
LBU 608a	Beach and bathers - from Bluff
LBU 608b	Same card listed as Asbury Park/Ocean Grove view
LBU 608c	Similar view as 608a
LBU 608d	Same card listed as Asbury Park/Ocean Grove view
LBU 609	Two young women in bathing suits on beach
LBU 610	Well dressed group of 14 in portrait on beach
LBU 611	Group of 15 in bathing suits at water's edge
LBU 612	Very large seated group in bathing suits
LBU 613	Dressed seated and standing group watching surf
LBU 614a	View of schooner and beach strollers (from Bluff)
LBU 614b	Similar view
LBU 615	One vessel off shore
LBU 616	Two vessels off shore
LBU 617	Three vessels on horizon
LBU 618	Five vessels on horizon

LBU 606 "President Grant at his Cottage by the Sea, Long Branch, N.J." Copyright 1872

The President and his family posed for G. W. Pach in this now famous photograph taken at Elberon. Grant's decision to make this part of Long Branch the site of the "summer White House" did much towards continuing the reputation of Long Branch as a lively and fashionable resort.

This original photographic enlargement of President Grant and his family was made (twenty years later) from one of the same negatives used to produce the stereograph on the opposite page. Signed by G. W. Pach in 1892 at his Lakewood Studio, this photograph attests to the enduring popularity of President Grant.

LBU 619	View of heavy surf
LBU 620	View of bathing ropes in quiet surf
LBU 621	"Colored Youth on the Beach at Long Branch"
LBU 622a	Informal group surrounding Life Saving Apparatus
LBU 622b	Very large formal group on beach (same area?)
LBU 623a	5th Maryland (N.G.?) Company
LBU 623b	Casual group of 15 N.G. soldiers in front of tent
LBU 623c	Nine soldiers in front of different tent
LBU 624	Charles Wardell's bath houses LB
LBU 625	Young America (also LITTLETON # 1274)
LBU 626	Three young girls in donkey cart
LBU 627	East End Hotel (label - no number)
LBU 628	Dr Prime's Cottage (label - no number)
LBU 629	View of residential area
LBU 630	Different view of residential area
LBU 631	Pach's Cottage, Chelsea Avenue
LBU 632	"Flying Cloud" cat boat at Pleasure Bay
LBU 633	"J. S. Abecasis Parlor Scene" OALB (yellow card)
LBU 634	"Cooper Cottage" West of Metropolitan Hotel
LBU 635	Wreck of the "Augustina" LB 1880
LBU 636	"Store Fronts" LB

LBU 633 "J. S. Abecasis Parlor Scene"

Here is a rare interior view taken in the home of J. S. Abecasis. This large, handsome Victorian cottage was located on Ocean Avenue, Long Branch, just north of the Pannaci Hotel, formerly Anthony Iauch's establishment.

LBU 635 Wreck of the "Augustina" at Long Branch, 1880

Pach's stereographic view of this particular stranded vessel is hardly dramatic. However, this less than exciting photo is an incredible link with a long forgotten moment in history. The demise of the Spanish brig "Augustina" and the rescue of the Captain and crew is a truly fascinating tale.

One of the worst New Jersey coastal storms in thirty years occurred on February 3, 1880. Responsible for the sinking of seven vessels between Sandy Hook and Long Branch, the ferocity of this violent winter storm was such that "the sea washed over the bluff into Ocean Avenue," Long Branch.

The "Augustina" left Havana, Cuba, on January 22nd bound for New York with a cargo of Spanish cedar. At 10:30 a.m., on February 3rd, the vessel grounded off Long Branch. Members of the U. S. Life Saving Service, fighting the storm tossed sea for two hours, had just rescued the Captain, his family, and the seven man crew of the three-masted schooner "E. E. Babcock" aground at Monmouth Beach. At that moment word came that the "Augustina" had also come ashore nearer Long Branch.

Quickly setting up rescue operations, the Life Saving Service made two attempts, by mortar, to attach a breeches buoy line to the stranded vessel. The seven man Italian crew was unfamiliar with the lifesaving apparatus. One of the rescuers finally swam to the ship, secured a line and five crew members were soon safely removed. The ocean became so violent that rescue operations for the last two crew members was halted until quieter seas prevailed at 1:00 p.m.

Through an interpreter, it was then discovered that Captain Antonio Andez had shot himself in the head when he saw the vessel was lost. The dying captain, found in his cabin, was taken ashore at Long Branch. Still alive a week later, he was removed to New York where he miraculously recovered.

A footnote to the story: The 120 foot mainmast of the "Augustina" was appropriated by John Hoey (owner of the Hollywood Hotel) and erected on "West Hill" – the highest elevation on his vast estate – and used as a flagpole!

J. C. Scott

A pioneer New Jersey photographer with a gallery at 11 Peace Street, New Brunswick, Scott advertised "Buildings Photographed and Stereoscopic Pictures Made to Order." By 1888, Scott's Studio was listed at 2 Peace Street while his residence was at 28 Paterson Street. Taken in the late 1860's, Scott's rare views of the Bay Shore Area are unique. These ten examples appear to have been issued as two series because of the duplication of catalogue numbers.

J. C. SCOTT VIEWS
1. "On the Beach at the Highlands"
2. "Steam Yacht Jennie"
2. "Shipyard - Billop's Point, Perth Amboy in distance"
3. "Steam Yacht Sarah"
4. "Hauling the Net"
4. "Highland Light House"
5. "Ready for Action at the Highlands"
6. "Big Fish Caught at Billop's Point" (Staten Island)
8. "All Hands on Deck. Preparing to Leave the Highlands"
9. "Return from a Bath. (beach scene)

No. 5.
Ready for Action at the Highlands.
PUBLISHED BY J. C. SCOTT.
Photograph Gallery at 11 Peace-Street, New-Brunswick, N. J.

J. C. Scott's label from stereo card # 5.

"No. 5. Ready for Action at the Highlands." 1869

This shipboard table's array of crabs, clams and strips of bait fish should be more than ample to produce a satisfactory catch. The extremely long fishing pole, the rifle and the small canon means this crew is REALLY ready for action!

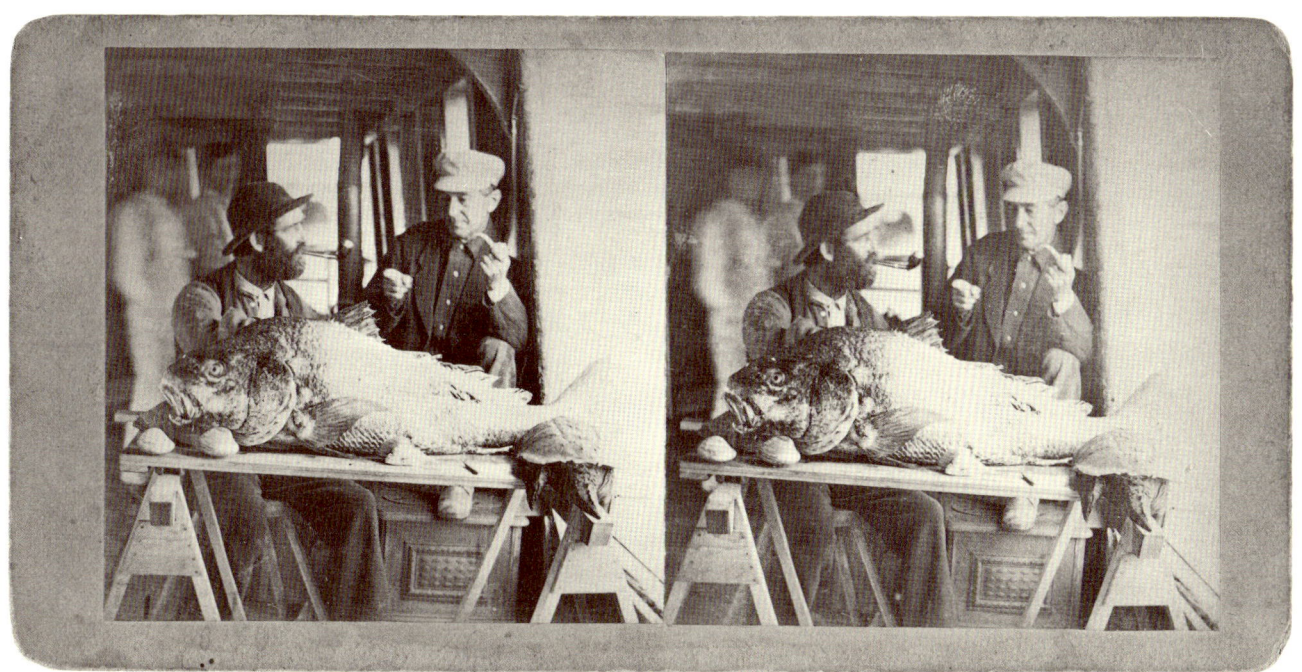

"No. 6. Big fish caught at Billops Point." 1869

Caught in the bay area near Staten Island, this hefty black drum was, indeed, a catch to be proud of.

Seth Shear and Shear Brothers

Both Seth Shear and Shear Brothers' local views remain a mystery even though we find "S. Shear, Out-Door Photographer. P.O. Box 208, Asbury Park, N. J." and "Shear Brothers: Landscape & Portrait Photos. Headquarters: Eatontown, N. J." To date none of their local stereographs have been found. Seven Shear stereo views have been noted but appear to be taken out of state. Seth Shear's Florida photographs are quite impressive.

Shear Brothers stereo card label. 1882

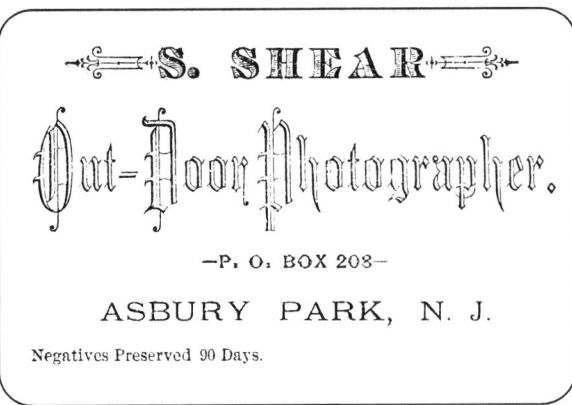

S. Shear stereo card label. 1885

An early Seth Shear label from his Florida studio.

William H. Stauffer

Although William H. Stauffer opened an Asbury Park studio in 1880 at 21 Cookman Avenue, he had been more than a successful "Portrait and Landscape Photographer" on East State Street, Trenton, for a decade before moving to the Jersey Shore. A popular and competent lensman, he was later to become the official photographer of Asbury Park's annual Baby Parade. The first one, incidentally, was held in July of 1890.

Numerous Stauffer photographs appeared in local publications of the period, particularly the "Sea Side Torch", a colorful Asbury Park magazine issued by the Pennypacker Press. Stauffer's later Gallery at 304 Cookman Avenue opposite the West End Hotel (near Wesley Lake) was certainly in the main flow of traffic thus enabling him, season after season, to photograph many local visitors. In 1897 Stauffer also had a small studio at 214 Broadway, Long Branch. By 1915 he relocated his Asbury Park studio to Cookman and Grand Avenue. Within a few years, however, he sold his business and quietly passed from the scene.

William H. Stauffer's early stereographs are of fine quality and are excellent documentary views. He may have produced almost one hundred stereographs of Monmouth County. Stauffer photographed most of his stereographic views at the Jersey Shore a number of years after Pach Brothers started their business in Long Branch. Most of Stauffer's cards are untitled and unnumbered. Nearby Lakewood, although in Ocean County, is part of the history of the Jersey Shore and for that reason Stauffer's (and other) significant early Lakewood stereo views are also noted.

Photographer William H. Stauffer, in wagon, poses outside of his Asbury Park Gallery in this 1892 illustration from the "Sea Side Torch." Stauffer was the official photographer for this magazine.

An early Asbury Park stereo view carried Stauffer's Trenton address on the back.

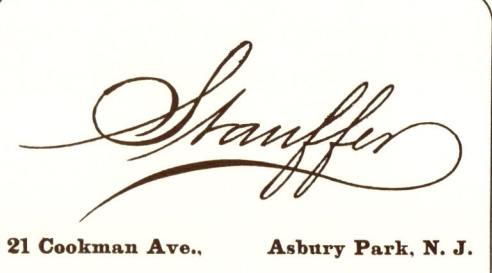

A typical Stauffer imprint found on his later stereo cards.

An interesting turn of the century caricature of Asbury Park Baby Parade photographer, William H. Stauffer.

WILLIAM H. STAUFFER VIEWS

ASBURY PARK VIEWS:
The following two grey cards have Stauffer's early "12 and 14 East State Street, Trenton, New Jersey" address on the reverse:
– "Pettingill's Cottage, Asbury Park. Dec 24,1880" Snow scene
– Ross Bathing Pavilion and beach

The following red cards have Stauffer's later "Asbury Park, N. J. Gallery - Cookman Ave. Opposite West End Hotel" address on the reverse:
– Gramercy House First and Bergh Avenues
– Gramercy House Similar view
– West End Hotel Kingsly and Asbury Avenues
– West End Hotel Snow scene
– Fifth Avenue Pavilion and beach
– Beach/Boardwalk south from foot of Second Avenue
– Ross Pavilion and bathers
– Crowded boardwalk scene
– Sunset Lake
– Deal Lake
– Large cottage
– Bosler Cottage
– Boarding House
– "Wreck of the Laura Bridgeman" Asbury Park. 1883
– "Wreck of the Laura Bridgeman" Later photo-session.

OCEAN GROVE VIEWS:
– Wesley Lake Westerly view of shore and boats
– Wesley Lake Distant westerly view
– Bathing at foot of Second Avenue
– Beach scene and fishing pier in distance
– Seven adults in beach scene August 2, 1881
– Large bathing group in surf
– Beach and boardwalk
– Beersheba Well
– Model of Jerusalem

LAKEWOOD (Ocean County) Views:
– General view of Lakewood
– Laurel House
– Rural street scene and store
– Pine Park
– Pine Woods
– Pine Avenue in Woods
– Lake Shore (Lake Carasaljo)
– Boat House (Lake Carasaljo)
– Boat House, Willow Landing, (Lake Carasaljo)
– Boat House (similar view)
– Hawk's Nest Bridge (Lake Carasaljo)
– Hawk's Nest Bridge (different view)

The following twelve early Lakewood views might have been taken by Stauffer. They are identified (in manuscript) as "Bricksburg now Lakewood, N.J."

Yellow Cards:
– Bricksburg Land Office
– Bird's-eye View of Bricksburg
– Single house in rural setting - Two boys on lawn
– Two houses in rural setting
– Long two story building
– Small group watching croquet game - "My friend's house"
– Close-up Brick walk and porch of "My friend's house"
– Dam and spillway
– Lake scene (of Willow Landing)
– Lake scene, wooden bridge, large building - warehouse?
– Lake scene, different bridge, man sitting by lake
– Lake scene, rowboat on shore
"No. 37 New Kent House, Lakewood"

These later views are of a much more developed Lakewood -
Pink Cards:
– Laurel House
– Residential street scene
– Large home, Gazebo and two girls
– Extremely large residence
– View of Lake Carasaljo - Boat House in distance

"Pettingill's Cottage, Asbury Park, N.J. Dec. 24, 1880"

This early Stauffer card is a rare view of the Jersey Shore - a wintery Asbury Park snow scene taken the day before Christmas one hundred and fifteen years ago.

Day and Brothers Ice Cream Saloon, Ocean Grove, N.J. 1882

Ice cream never tasted better that at this quaint Ocean Grove Victorian landmark.

Gramercy House, Asbury Park, N.J. 1882

William H. Stauffer, like G. W. Pach, found ready sales in stereo views of guest-laden hotel porches. Over two hundred hotels, boarding houses and cottages in Ocean Grove and Asbury Park have been photographed by the stereo camera.

"Wreck of the Laura Bridgeman." 1883

On her way from Baltimore to Fall River, the Schooner *Laura Bridgeman* was wrecked off Third Avenue, Asbury Park on June 19, 1883.

Wreck of the Laura Bridgeman" 1883

The remains of the *Laura Bridgeman's* broken hull was photographed many weeks later. It was a curiosity that attracted many visitors for the remainder of the summer.

Underwood & Underwood

New York, London, Toronto, Canada.
Works and Studios: Arlington, N.J., Littleton, N.H., Washington, D.C.

This well-known stereo publishing firm started in business in 1882 and became a giant in the industry. After having produced almost 40,000 titles by 1920, the rights and remaining stereo viewcards of Underwood & Underwood were obtained by the Keystone View Company in 1923.

UNDERWOOD & UNDERWOOD VIEWS

– "Sir Thomas Lipton on Steam Yacht ERIN watching SHAMROCK 11 at Sandy Hook, 1901"

– "Little Mother's Day - Doll Parade at Asbury Park, N.J., 1901"

5507. "Neptune's Smiles - Old Ocean's playful dashing breakers, on the Beach, Asbury Park, N.J., U.S.A., 1901"

– *"Little Mother's Day - Doll Parade at Asbury Park, N.J., 1901"*

The Doll Parade and the Baby Parade were, for years, two of Asbury Park's festive summer events.

Peter F. Weil

The name Philip F. Weil listed in various New York City Directories (1866-68) as a photographer at 202 Fulton Street, apparently was that of a relative (or possibly an error in listing) of Peter F. Weil whose studio in 1870 was at 643 Broadway. Like nost New York City photographers in business for some time, Weil continued to move his studio uptown as the city expanded. By 1875 his studio was at 685 Broadway. Weil bought a number of stereographs from other photographers and reissued them under his own name. Weil published at least two Monmouth County views. These views, however, were taken between 1870 and 1874 by G. W. Pach of Long Branch.

PETER F. WEIL VIEWS

– "View of the Ocean from Long Branch" (same photo-session as Pach # 26 and # 78)
– "Boat Scene at Sea Bright Near Long Branch" (Pach # 113)

– *"Boat Scene at Sea Bright Near Long Branch"*

G.W. Pach captured this leisurely moment a century and a quarter ago. A tomboy wades in the water while her prim companions wistfully wait for an invitation for a boat ride on the Shrewsbury River. In the left background is Rumson and to the right, faintly in the distance, is the Highlands of Navesink.

H. C. White Co.

Chicago, New York, London.
Gen'l Office and Works, North Bennington, Vt., U.S.A.
The "Perfec" Stereograph Patented April 14, 1903.

Starting just before the turn of the century and for almost fifteen years, H. C. White & Company published a great number of quality views covering a wide variety of subjects. There are at least four views of Monmouth County interest. The Keystone View Company acquired White's negatives by 1915.

H. C. WHITE AND COMPANY VIEWS

427. "The Child of the Sea. One of the floats in the baby parade. Asbury Park, N.J., U.S.A." 1907

428. "Royal Pair on a Barrel Throne, baby parade, Asbury Park, N.J., U.S.A." 1907

429. "The Arrival of the Stork. A unique float in the baby parade. Asbury Park, N.J., U.S.A." 1907

18. "A Holiday in New York - Excursion Steamers going up the Harbor, New York." 1908

18. "A Holiday in New York - Excursion Steamers going up the Harbor, New York. 1908"

The flag-flying Steamer *St. John* was one of the early Central Rail Road of New Jersey boats that ran between New York and Sandy Hook to connect with the Central Rail Road's trains bound for Long Branch.

167

C. W. Woodward

From Rochester, New York, G. W. Woodward published a vast amount of stereographic views from the early 1870's through the 1880's. Many of his cards were copies. Some of his Monmouth County views were taken by Colwell Lane's New Jersey Stereographic View Company (and others possibly taken by G. W. Pach.) Lane's views appear to be prints from the original negatives...(acquired by Woodward)? The Union View Company of Rochester was the successor to Woodward and issued many of his cards. The various "series" that were published by Woodward are, truthfully, quite confusing. Many of the same cards were issued in these different series. For example:

G. W. WOODWARD VIEWS

"New York City and Vicinity" series
   1408. The Atlantic from Long Branch
   1410. On the Beach at Long Branch

"N. Y. City and Central Park" series
   1410. On the Beach at Long Branch

Union View Company, Rochester
   1410. On the Beach at Long Branch

1410. On the Beach at Long Branch

> Looking northward from the Bluff, beyond the bath houses, a sign proclaims "Bathing Suits to let. Pay in advance."

The following cards, although not identified as to publisher, appear to be other series issued by Woodward.

"New York City and Central Park" series. Yellow card
    1410. On the Beach at Long Branch

"American Scenery - New York City and Vicinity" series
    1436. Club House (Monmouth Park), Long Branch

"American Scenery - American Scenery" series. Yellow cards
    1410. On the Beach at Long Branch
    1435. "Lake" - Wesley Lake-Fairy Island, Ocean Grove

AMERICAN SCENERY, MARINE series. Yellow cards

Most of the items in this series are from New Jersey Stereoscopic View Company negatives. Labels on the backs of the AMERICAN SCENERY, MARINE stereo cards are minor catalogs of Cape Ann and Nahant, Mass., and Long Branch views. There are over twenty monmouth County views in this series.

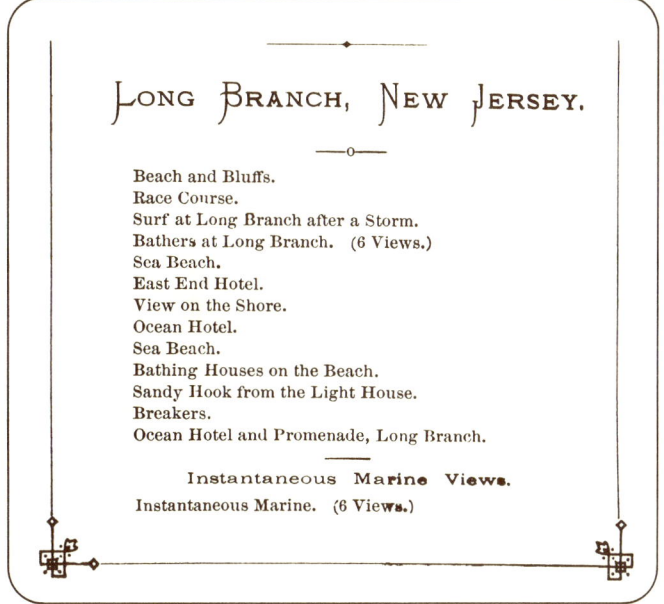

–"Race Course" (Monmouth Park, Long Branch, N.J.)

An early view captures Monmouth Park's Grandstand, Judges Stand and the finish line of this popular New Jersey race track. Eight other stereographic views of Monmouth Park have been noted.

AMERICAN SCENERY Yellow card

(71) "Drawbridge Near the Highlands" (is New Jersey Stereographic View Company card #53).

The label on the back of this particular 4 x 7 "de luxe" size card lists only Baltimore and Philadelphia views. See page 109.

Unknown Photographers and Publishers

There are more than a dozen significant early Monmouth County stereographic views without any identification as to photographer or publisher. These cards possibly represent the work of three or four camermen. It is possible a few of these views were taken by G. W. Pach.

YELLOW CARDS 1866 - 1869

- Congress Hall Hotel, Long Branch 1866
- Surf at Long Branch
- Ocean Hotel, Long Branch

469. The Wallack Group on Cottage Porch, Long Branch
826. The Wallack Cottage, Long Branch

- G. W. Childs' Cottage, Long Branch
- Steamer *Neversink*, Navesink River

GREEN CARD

- Steamer *Long Branch*, Horseshoe Cove, Sandy Hook

The following YELLOW card and the following RED cards were published in the early 1870's and the late 1880's. The cards are various size cabinet stereographs.

YELLOW CARD

- Wesley Lake, Ocean Grove and Ocean

RED CARDS

- Coleman House, Asbury Park
- Sunset Lake, Grand Avenue Ferry, Asbury Park
- Inlet. Highland Beach   1889

Other Monmouth County views were issued by the following minor or little known publishers:

"American Stereoscopic Company"

"European and American Views"

"Stereographic Gems of American and Foreign Scenery"

Steamer LONG BRANCH
Photographer unknown

Under the control of Col. James Fisk and Jay Gould the *Long Branch* serviced the New Jersey Southern Railroad Company sailing between New York City and Horseshoe Cove, Sandy Hook from 1870 to 1874.

"Inlet. Highland Beach After Storm. Sept. 1889"
Photographer unknown.   Rutgers University Library

Dramatic evidence of a major coastal storm. At this location the old Sandy Hook Inlet was reopened for two weeks as a result of the ocean's onslaught.

American Stereoscopic Company

In business for more than a decade around the turn of the century, the American Stereoscopic Company of 853 Broadway, New York, published many different views. The Company was particularly known for its tinted stereographs. The majority of these were executed by R.Y. Young. To date, only on Monmouth County view has been noted.

> **AMERICAN STEREOSCOPIC COMPANY VIEWS**
> - "Spruce Avenue, Hoey's Grounds, Long Brance, U.S.A." tinted view.

– *"Spruce Avenue, Hoey's Grounds, Long Branch,U.S.A."*
    An uninspired view of Mr. Frederick Hoey's magnificent gardens.

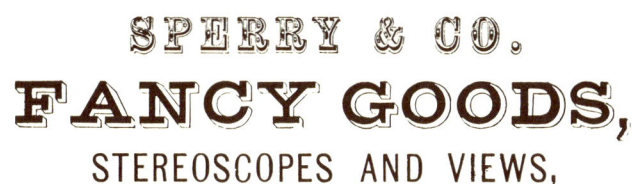

1898

A Sperry & Co. advertising card with reference to the American Stereoscopic Company.

European and American Views

The name of the photographer and/or publisher of this card has not been identified at this time. The card appears to be a reissue or a pirated view published in the 1890's.

> **EUROPEAN AND AMERICAN VIEWS**
> "–045. The Surf, Asbury Park"

"–045. The Surf, Asbury Park"

In the distance one can even see bathers in the surf at Ocean Grove.

STEREOGRAPHIC GEMS
of American and Foreign Scenery

The photographer and/or publisher of this stereo card remains unidentified at this time.

> **STEREOGRAPHIC GEMS of American and Foreign Scenery Views**
> "3407a. Steamship St. Paul. Stranded at Long Branch, N.J., Jan. 25, 1896."

"3407a. Steamship St. Paul. Stranded at Long Branch, N.J., Jan. 25, 1896."

This is possibly the best stereograhic view of the stranded Steamer *St. Paul*. Two hundred and sixty-three passengers and crew were safely removed from the vessel along with one million dollars in gold. The *St. Paul* remained aground until February 5th when it was finally towed offshore.

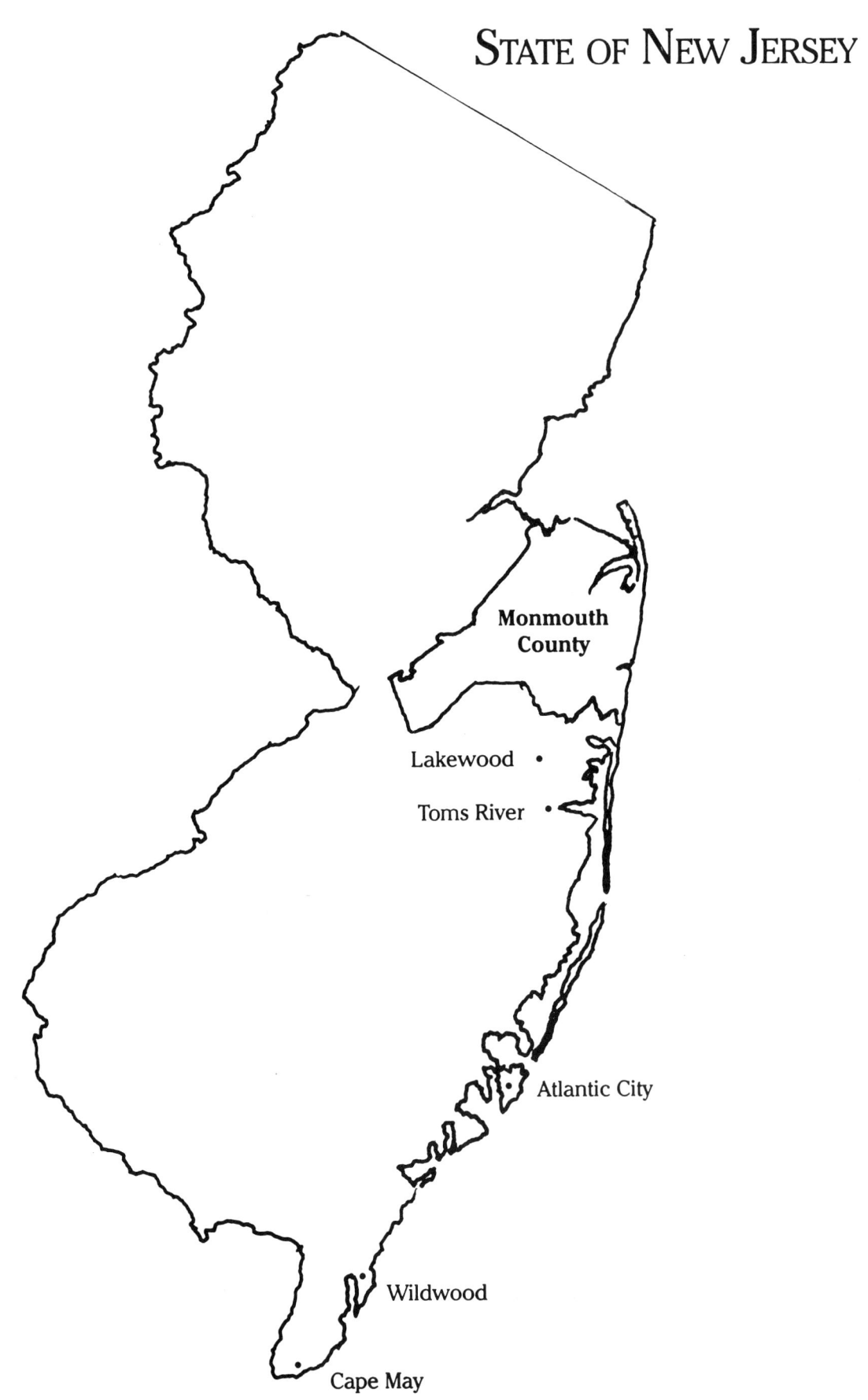

South Jersey Shore Stereographic List

The following list includes stereographs of Toms River, Wildwood, Atlantic City, and Cape May in the Moss Archives. It is merely a token list and records only a fraction of the many views, taken in the past, that document this southern portion of the Jersey Shore. There are probably at least a thousand different stereographs of just Atlantic City and the Cape May area. The majority of Atlantic City's views are of the beach, various bathing scenes and views of the famous Boardwalk. Early beach scenes and Cape May hotels are well documented in stereographs of the 1870's.

ATLANTIC CITY VIEWS

AMERICAN STEREOSCOPIC COMPANY
725-727 Broadway, New York
Grey card: Copyright 1901 by R. Y Young
– "By the Sad Sea Waves, Atlantic City, N.J."

BERRY, KELLEY & CHADWICK, Publishers,
Philadelphia, U.S.A.
Grey card: Series of 1906 by E. W. Kelley
– "Youthful "Pardners" in the Surf, Atlantic City, N.J."

EXCELSIOR STEREO. VIEWS
(Sold by Universal Photo. Art Co.)
Cream card: by W. M. Chase
– "Down by the Sea, Atlantic City, N.J."
– "Down by the Sea. Atlantic City, N.J."
  (Two different views)

S. R. FISHER
Stereoscopic and Landscape Photographer
Norristown, Pa.
Pink card: Cabinet Size
    "Instantaneous Views in and around Atlantic City, N. J."
115. Beach Scene
191. Hotel, surf & seawall
– Traymore Hotel

GRIFFITH & GRIFFITH
Philadelphia, Pa.

American & Foreign Views
Yellow card:
– "Atlantic City, In The Surf."

Pink card: 1902 series. Geo. W. Griffith, Publisher
2679. "Watching the Bathers, Atlantic City, N.J."
2692. "A Pleasant Sail at the Inlet, Atlantic City, N.J."
2697. "Knee Deep. Atlantic City."

Grey card: 1905 series. By Griffith & Griffith. Geo. W. Griffith, Publisher
2678. "The New Boardwalk. Looking South. Atlantic City."

Yellow card: Sold only by Griffith & Griffith. William H. Rau, Photographer, Philadelphia, Pa.
7947. "Atlantic City, Crowded Boardwalk, (South)."
7949. "Atlantic City, Crowded Boardwalk, (North)."
10463. "Atlantic City, A Belle (W)ringing Wet."

Yellow card: Sold only by Griffith & Griffith. H. L Roberts & Co., Photographers, Philadelphia, Pa.
– "Bathers at Atlantic City."

INTERNATIONAL STEREOSCOPIC VIEW CO.
New York City, U.S.A.

Grey card:
– "Atlantic City. A Beach Study."

INTERNATIONAL VIEW COMPANY
Home Office and Works, Decatur, Illinois, U.S.A.

Grey card: Copyright 1901 by C. L. Wasson.
727. "All the World a Bathing Goes. Atlantic City, N.J."

J. F. JARVIS, Publisher
Washington, D.C.
Sold only by Underwood & Underwood

Cream card: Copyright 1890 by J. F. Jarvis
– "Sunday Morning on the Board Walk, Atlantic City, N.J., U.S.A."

Cream card: Copyright 1891 by J. F. Jarvis
– "Sunday Morning on the Board Walk, Atlantic City, N.J., U.S.A." (same photo-session as above.)
– "We Love to Bathe in the Ocean Wave, Atlantic City, New Jersey, U.S.A."
– "We Love to Bathe in the Ocean Wave, Atlantic City, New Jersey, U.S.A." (different view than above.)
– "A Delightful Surf, Atlantic City, New Jersey, U.S.A."
– "Atlantic City's Crowded Beach, New Jersey, U.S.A."
— "Life in the Ocean Wave, Atlantic City, N.J., U.S.A."

Cream card: Copyright 1896 by J. F. Jarvis
– "A Salvation Army Service on the Beach, Atlantic City, New Jersey, U.S.A."
– "Atlantic City's Crowded Beach, New Jersey, U.S.A."
– "The Grand Old Ocean, Atlantic City, New Jersey, U.S.A."

E. W. KELLEY, Publisher
Studio and Home Office, Chicago, U.S.A.

Grey Card: Copyright 1903 by William H. Rau
599. "In the Good Old Summertime." Atlantic City

KEYSTONE VIEW COMPANY
Meadville, Pa.,

Cream card:Copyright 1899: B. L Singley
0688. "A Cake Walk on the Beach, Atlantic City, N.J."

Grey card:
1007-60. "In the Surf, Atlantic City, N. J."
1007-60. "In the Surf, Atlantic City, N. J." - different views.
26495-T19. "Summer Crowds at America's Foremost Seaside Resort, Atlantic City, New Jersey."
29406-T60. "Summer Crowds at America's Foremost Seaside Resort, Atlantic City, N.J." - different view.
29444-60. "In the Surf, Atlantic City, N. J." - different than 1007-60 views above.
29576-T30. "Summer Crowds at America's Foremost Seaside Resort, Atlantic City, New Jersey." - different view than 26495-T19 and 29406-T60 above.
32837-20. "Atlantic City, N. J., America's Foremost Seaside Resort - the Boardwalk and Steel Pier from the Breakers Hotel."
A number of the above views are from boxed sets.

"Photographed and Published by
B. W. KILBURN,
Littleton, N.H."

Cream card:Copyright 1888:
4780. "Life in the Ocean Wave."
4781. "At Home on the Rolling Beach."

Copyright 1891:
6759. "The Merry Bathers, Atlantic City."
6771. "One Hours Catch, Atlantic City."
6772. "The Inlet, Atlantic City."

Copyright 1897: James M. Davis, distributor.
11412. "Seeking Health from Mother Earth, Atlantic City."
11836. "Wringing Wet, Atlantic City, N.J."
11843. "When My Ship Comes In, Atlantic City, N.J."
11845. "Teaching Jack new tricks, Atlantic City, N.J."
11846. "The multitude by the Sea, Atlantic City, N.J."
11848. "Go look to the east, Go look to the west, Go choose the one you love the best. Atlantic City, N.J."
11849. "Great is our fun when the tide comes in., Atlantic City, N.J."

Copyright 1903:
15872. "With his best girl, on the beach, Atlantic City, N.J."
15877. "The lone bather, Atlantic City, N.J."
15879. "Hoky-poky ice-cream, Atlantic City, N.J."

Photographed by
R. NEWELL
724 Arch St., Philadelphia

Green card:
– "Sea Breeze House. Atlantic City."

HARRY PHILLIPS, Photographer
Yellow cards: Atlantic City Views - '82
1122. "The Dennis Cottage (for Guests of the Fortescue House)."
1124. "The Light House."

WM. RUTHERFORD, Photographer
Hammonton, N.J.

Red card: Atlantic City Views
– "Surf House"
– "Penna. Ave. - towards Sea."

STANDARD SERIES
Cream card:
– "Crowded Beach. Atlantic City."
– "Atlantic City. A Splashing."

STEREO PHOTO CO., Publishers
Dolgeville, N.Y., U.S.A.

77. "Crowded Beach. Atlantic City"

STEREOSCOPIC GEMS
OF AMERICAN and FOREIGN SCENERY
Universal Series

Grey card:
2911. "Atlantic City, Goat Carriage on the Beach"
4376. "Atlantic City, in the Surf (from the Pier)."

STROHMEYER & WYMAN, Publishers
New York
Sold only by Underwood & Underwood

Cream card: Copyright 1891 by Strohmeyer & Wyman
– "Summer Sports, Atlantic City, N.J., U.S.A."

UNDERWOOD & UNDERWOOD, Publishers
New York, London, Toronto, Canada & Ottawa, Kansas

Cream card: Copyright 1896 by J. F. Jarvis
– "Atlantic City's Crowded Beach, New Jersey, U.S.A."
Grey card:
– (untitled. Same as "A Delightful Surf" by Jarvis, 1891)
– (untitled. Ocean Bathers.)
1906 Series: from boxed sets
5500. "Life on the Ocean Wave, Atlantic City, New Jersey, U.S.A."
10707. "Palatial hotels and crowded promenades (s.) along the beach, Atlantic City, N.J."

THE UNIVERSAL PHOTO ART COMPANY
Philadelphia, Pa.

C. H. Graves, Publisher

Cream card:
2912. "Atlantic City, On the Beach."
4373. "Scene on the Boardwalk, Atlantic City."

Grey card:
Art Nouveau (Platino) Stereograph. Copyright 1903 by C. H. Graves.
4390. "Beach Scene at Bathing Hour. Atlantic City, N.J."

Copyright 1902 by C. H. Graves:
4392. "Atlantic City at the height of the season."

UNIVERSAL VIEW COMPANY
William H. Rau, Publisher, Philadelphia, U.S.A.

Cream card:
– "Float Me Charlie." Atlantic City

Grey card: "Copyrighted 1903 by William H. Rau."
– "A Beach Beauty Basking in the Sand, Atlantic City, N.J."
– "A Big Sunday on the Beach, A Summer Playground for Countless Thousands, Atlantic City, N.J."
– "Among the Crowd on the Beach. Atlantic City."

H. C. WHITE Co., Publishers.
North Bennington, Vt.

Cream card: 1899
– "The Beach, from Boardwalk, Atlantic City, N.J."

The "Perfec" Stereograph. Patented April 14, 1903.
Grey card: Copyright 1901 by H. C. White Co.
475. "The Crowded Beach, Atlantic City, N.J."

The "Perfec" Stereograph. EDITION de LUXE.
  Patented April 14, 1903.
Grey card: Copyright 1901 by H. C. White Co.
476. "The Bathers, Atlantic City, N.J."
477. "The Beach, from the Board Walk, Atlantic City, N.J."
479. "A Jolly Crowd, Atlantic City, N.J."

TOMS RIVER VIEWS

CHARLES BERRIEN
Toms River, N. J. Ocean County

– Kitten in farm basket near barn
– A dog and two cats in yard near barn

PRICES' PHOTOGRAPHIC GALLERY
Toms River N.J. Ocean County
"South Jersey Views"

– Victorian Home
– Interior scene of Tabernacle (?) and Minister

WILDWOOD VIEWS

UNIVERSAL PHOTO ART CO.
The Art Nouveau (Platino) Stereograph
C. H. Graves, Publisher, Phila., USA

4389. "A Yacht Race at Wildwood, N.J." 1905

CAPE MAY VIEWS

J. B. BROWN
Foot of Ocean Street, Cape May City   Cape May County

– Street scene. Ivey's Dry Good House and "New Cottage"

CHESTER & HANDY, Photographers
S.W. Cor. Stockton Hotel Bath Houses
Beach Ave. & Ocean Street,. Cape May, N.J. Cape May County
Branch of 427 7th St., N.W., Washington, D.C.
Groups Photographed Instantaneously Under the Sky Light

– Small group of children and ladies posed on hotel porch
– Larger group, mostly children, on hotel porch
– Street scene and Westmoreland Villa

JAMES CREMER
18 South Eighth St., Philadelphia

– Knights Templar's Pilgrimage to Cape May, August 18th, 1874.
  (Seventy-five members posed on a staircase and balcony.)

HENRY H. HALL, Photographer
Sea Grove, N.J. Cape May County

Cabinet size:
– View from Cape May Light House   1876
– USLSS Station # 40 Light House in distance   1876
– Hotel   1876

Published by
E. F. HOVEY, Ag't.
1226 Chestnut Street, Philadelphia, Pa.
and for sale exclusively by ASA HULL,
at the "ARCADE", Cape May, N.J.

– J. H. Benezet & Bros. Tinware and Stove Depot. Jackson St.

L. D. JOHNSON
Vineland, N. J.
"Cape May Views"
– McMakin's Atlantic Hotel. Children with covered goat cart. Jackson St.

W. LONG, Photographer
Cape May County
Congress Hall Lawn
Cape May, N. J. and 1632 North 13th St., Phila.

– Musicians and audience on porch of large hotel
– Crowd on same porch of large hotel
– Close-up of large group on porch. Different hotel
– Surf scene. Bathers and steamer
– Light House and lake
– Cottage of R. A. Packer

R. NEWELL & Co.
626 and 724 Arch Street, Philadelphia
also
R. NEWELL & SON
General Business Photographers
"American Views"

– Cape May Hotel
– Hotel at Cape May
511 Beach scene. Horse and wagon, bathers
– Beach scene. Horses and wagons, bathers
– Distant beach scene
– Surf scene
– Surf scene (green card)

WILLIAMS
Cape May, N.J. Cape May County
Late with BRADY of Washington, D.C.

– Stockton House, Beach Ave. between Howard and Gurney
– Hotel interior. Large Dining Room
– Surf scene. Schooners and steamer off shore
– Beach scene. Similar boats in distance

O.H. WILLARD, Photographer
Cape May County
Congress Hall Lawn, Cape May, N.J.
and 1206 Chestnut Street, Phila.

– Willard's Photographic tent on Congress Hall Lawn with children playing croquet
– Atlantic Hotel. Jackson St.
– Columbia Hotel. Decatur and Ocean
– Stockton House. Beach Ave. between Howard and Gurney
– Large crowd on hotel porch
– Centennial Pier
– Boardwalk/Beach scene with paddle wheel steamer
– Four bathers in surf
– Fifteen bathers in surf. Steamer off shore
– Hundreds of bathers in surf
– Steam yacht off shore
– Schooner off shore
– Similar scene. Green card
– Breaking waves

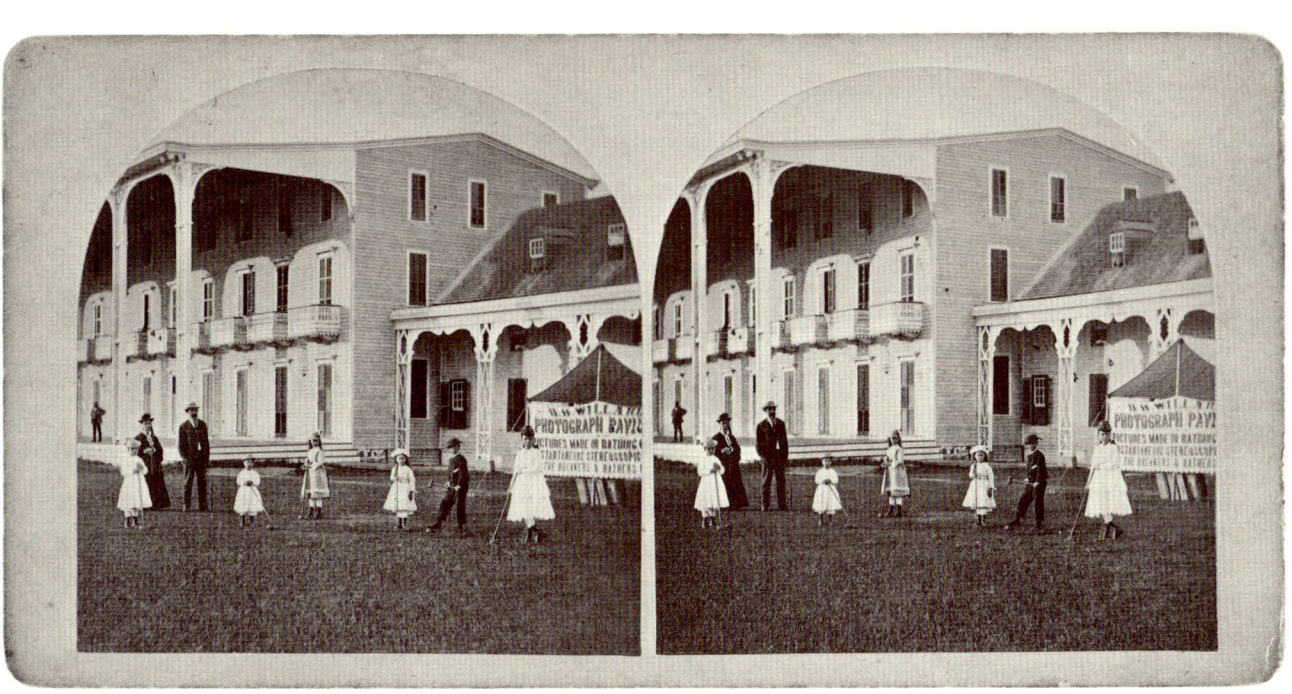

BIBLIOGRAPHY

Darrah, William C., "Stereo Views. A History of Stereographs in America and Their Collection." Times and News Publishing Co., Gettysburg, Pa., 1964.

Darrah, William C., "The World of Stereographs." W. C. Darrah, Pub., Gettysburg, Pa., 1977.

Gernsheim, Helmut & Alison, "A Concise History of Photography." Grosset & Dunlap, N. Y., 1965.

Humphrey, S. D., "A Practical Manual of the Collodion Process, Giving in Detail a Method for Producing Positive and Negative Pictures on Glass and Paper." Humphrey's Journal, N.Y., 1857.

Moss Jr., George H., "Double Exposure. Early Stereographic Views of Historic Monmouth County, New Jersey, and Their Relationship to Pioneer Photography." Ploughshare Press, Sea Bright, N.J., 1971.

Newhall, Beaumont, "Latent Image, The Discovery of Photography." Anchor Books, (Paperback Edition) Garden City, N.Y., 1967.

Newhall, Beaumont, "The Daguerreotype in America." New York Graphic Society, N.Y., 1968.

Price, Henry Clay, "How To Make Pictures: Easy Lessons for the Amateur Photographer." Scovill Manufacturing Co., N.Y., 1882.

Rinhart, Floyd & Marion, "American Daguerreian Art." Clarkson N. Potter, N.Y., 1967.

Taft, Robert, "Photography and the American Scene." Dover Publications, Inc., N.Y., 1964 Ed.

Waldsmith, John, "Stereo Views. An Illustrated History and Price Guide." Wallace-Homestead Book Co., Radnor, Pa., 1991.

Wilson, Edward L., "Wilson's Photographics: A Series of Lessons Accompanied by Notes, On All the Processes Which are Needful in the Art of Photography." E. L. Wilson, Philadelphia, Pa., 1883.

"The Philadelphia Photographer." E. L. Wilson, Editor. Benerman & Wilson, Philadelphia, Pa., 1871, Vol. V111 and 1876, Vol. X111.

NOTES

*Book Design, Typography
and Production*
WILFRED D. HOWITT

Printed by
THE RIVERVIEW PRESS
Little Silver, NJ